William Simpson
Happy Memories

‘Uncle Willie’

70 years of unbroken congregational ministry

ISBN 0 947 848 11 8

First published 1995
by Caron Publications
Peak Press Building
Eccles Road
Chapel-en-le-Frith
Derbyshire SK12 6RQ

Typeset and printed
in England by
THE PEAK PRESS COMPANY
Chapel-en-le-Frith
Derbyshire

‘Uncle Willie’

70 years of unbroken congregational ministry

by

Don Borland

It is when you give of yourself that you truly give.

Work is love made visible.

Kahlil Gibran - *The Prophet*

Chapel-en-le-Frith

For Lorna - the other great enabler

To the friends of Willie Simpson in the churches in which he has served throughout his ministry.

Acknowledgments

I am grateful for the practical support and encouragement which I have had from Dennis and Rosie Harding, particularly in the early research stages. Were it not for them this book would not now be in being.

My thanks go to Will Newman for the line drawing on the title page, to Frank Nixon, the head of Chinley School, for information relating to the history of the school, and to Alan Watson for permission to use the photograph of Chinley School, 1902.

My wife, Lorna, one of the two great enablers in my life (the other one is Willie), has shown great patience and enthusiasm, qualities which sit well together in her, and has been a very sharp-eyed editor. Bill Ryecroft, John Stott and Tony Greenslade have read the manuscript and have given me good advice on the matters of both content and expression, for which I thank them all. So, too, did Roger Fowler, my friend of many years and my best man when I married Lorna in Chinley Chapel. Roger died last year, but not before he made the acquaintance of Willie in the manuscript. I am glad that one good friend, a real character, met another good friend, a real character.

PREFACE

The suggestion to write this life of Rev. Dr. William Simpson came from Dennis Harding, a Trustee of Chinley Chapel, during the tea interval of a cricket match between Buxworth Second Team and Stockport Sunday School. Buxworth, for whom we were both playing, had batted first and had performed miserably, being all out for sixty runs. There was little left to compete for in the match for Buxworth. However, for me, the attraction of the task Dennis had mooted, the sheer excitement lent by the idea, put wings on feet in a way totally unwarranted by the state of the match. Nevertheless, inevitably, we lost, and fairly quickly, but I had begun a journey which is by no means over with the completion of this biography.

The first stage of the journey was to ask Willie himself if he would agree to my undertaking an account of his life. On the day that I visited him to propose a biography, he had just received the draft of an article about him by a writer, Jack Hanmer, for a local newspaper, the High Peak Courier. As I recall, this painted a very authentic likeness of Willie. Significantly and, I hoped, propitiously for me at that moment, the article ended with the words, 'The full story will one day simply have to be told.' This was almost too much of a co-incidence!

However, after two weeks of consideration Willie said that he felt that he could not agree. There were some poignant, even painful, memories he was reluctant to bring up. Naturally I was disappointed, but decided that I should do some of the preparatory research anyway. I thought it proper that I should tell him that I was doing so. This proved to be helpful to my cause. Willie changed his mind. He thought that to co-operate would ensure that I should hear his side of the story too! And so here are the fruits of several years of friendship and sharing and privilege, the privilege of getting to know very closely a remarkable human being.

Willie Simpson's life is remarkable for several reasons. First, even these days it is not very usual to live for almost ninety-seven years. Second, there must be very few eighty-year-olds, let alone ninety-year-olds, who sustain their energy and vitality enough to continue in their calling actively for seventy years, and that does not include his years of training and preparation. Third, and most important, is the manner of service, the devotion, optimism and unjudging acceptance of people, whatever their persuasion - in other words, the love and the faith. It is very important to Willie that he can end a day feeling that it is a 'day's work well done'. At this stage of his life one may feel that he is entitled to rest and resist the drive to work. But that is what he does not want. That would remove his raison d'etre. So, it seems reasonable to speculate that he will continue this habit of a very long lifetime until his time comes. At which point I can imagine the keeper of the gates of heaven saying to Willie, 'I'm all the better for seeing you, my dear.'

Writing this life has been a great pleasure. Beyond the friendship it has given me with Willie himself, it has brought me into contact with many people whose recollections have been a potent mixture of pleasure and poignancy, who have had in common a warmth and a sense of amusement, love and admiration for Willie. I am grateful for the opportunity to meet them. I hope this picture compares adequately with the picture they carry in their memories of the man.

Had it not been for Gladys Shirt of Combs who suggested Chinley Chapel to Lorna and me as a church to be married in, the trail would not have begun which has led to the writing of this biography. Belonging to Chinley Chapel brought me into contact with Willie Simpson. It also brought me fellowship, kindness, welcome and love - this church has come to have the same kind of place in my heart as it does in Willie's (perhaps not quite the same - I shall never have the years!). The church flourishes now, a tribute both to the way Willie set it on its feet again, and to the current Minister and his wife, Rev. Bill and Betty Bentham (Willie said he thought no-one would ever be as good a minister's wife as his own Ida, but 'Betty has proved me wrong.'). So I must thank Bill and Chinley Chapel for taking Lorna, me and Kate, my daughter, into the fold, and opening up a wealth of God-given opportunity.

The Rev. Dr. William Simpson D. D., 1995.

William Simpson, aged 10, 1908

1

An Earnest Young Man

Rev. Dr. William Simpson in his nineties has all the vigour of mind and bearing of a man in his sixties. He sits on the dining chair, which was a parting present from his congregation at Mexborough in south Yorkshire, at the table in the window overlooking the back garden at 20, New Road, Buxworth. It is only when he has to get out of the chair that the stiffness of old age is visible. But then the movement is quick and purposeful, a kind of scurrying shuffle that brooks no delay, whether to answer the telephone or a knock at the door, or to find a piece of memorabilia. The besetting problem is deafness, alleviated to some extent by a hearing aid. But like all the problems that William Simpson has faced in life, this is made light of. It is something to be contended with and got round. He can hear better on the telephone than in normal conversation. Making arrangements and appointments with him over the phone is remarkably easy and he has never kept an appointments diary in his life, even at his busiest as a minister of large and thriving congregations. He has carried all his commitments in his head and has never failed to keep them. Everyone who has dealt with him in any sphere marvels at his memory, especially for time and date and place.

William Simpson's abiding love is people. He has always been gregarious, affable, and gentle in approach. But there is no doubting his strength of purpose, especially in situations which need confronting. There was an occasion when a man had been salting away church funds for his own needs. Willie tackled this with compassion for the man and for his family, ensuring that the man could restore to the church what had been lost and resisting the impulse among members of the church to punish. Best of all, the man and his family remained in the church for the rest of their lives.

There is no doubt that being a minister gave him the centre-stage which he loves. Throughout his life there has been a strain of eccentricity, which in his younger days made him a figure of fun, but which, as he matured as a minister he may well have cultivated, and turned to good effect. He never appears without his dog collar and has always dressed with a degree of formality. In his view the minister of the church never has a day off.

Ask people who have known Rev. Dr. William Simpson at some time in his long, long life why he has occupied such a bright place in their memories and they recall his courage, his unequivocal faith in God through Jesus Christ, his sublime ability to lead by example and his optimism. They remember him, with smiles of both admiration and indulgence, as an extravert and an eccentric. They think of his earnestness and his unswerving devotion. They remember his unaffected delight in people and especially the public persona - which he may also have cultivated - the black-clad, be-hatted idiosyncrasy on a bicycle, the very antithesis of earnestness. Earnestness is not the most inspiring of human virtues. It is associated with steadiness and reliability, with quiet, even dogged, determination, admirable attributes, for sure, but not the stuff of charisma and flamboyance. And yet when the earnest William Simpson came into a room no-one had any doubt that he was there.

William Simpson is a man composed of a paradox, a series of paradoxes, the tension of which generates our impulse simply to be, to live. William Simpson at ninety-six years of age lives, in the full sense of the word. His physical energy is in decline, his physical faculties dimmed; memory and mental faculties are hardly diminished. This day, next Sunday, next week, the next Special Occasion for his church are the focus - all belonging in the present and the future. The past is learned from, sometimes celebrated, but the future summons, calls him on, energises. Optimism sustains him. He has always been like that. His mother taught him that that was the way to be.

A photograph at the age of ten speaks of his earnestness. He looks sturdy, four-square. Through the spectacles which he has worn from an early age the deep-set blue eyes gaze with an immense steadiness at the camera. The brow is unfurrowed to the point of serenity and has remained so throughout his life. The facial set, the sense of purpose, the immovability, are the same at ten as they were to be at ninety. He seems hardly ever to have been a child. His focus was not other children; rather, it was humanity in general. He did not feel the impulse to play. More, he wished to work, to meet, to talk, to help, to get things done, to bring about improvement. As a child, by modern standards he was slow to mature physically. Food was neither plentiful nor as nutritious as it is nowadays. Nevertheless William Simpson had robust health throughout his childhood and grew steadily, his round features and fair, wiry hair expressing the rural Derbyshire and Lincolnshire of his forbears.

Chinley, a village on the southern edge of the Dark Peak, came to prominence in the late nineteenth century. A large railway station was built there as a focal point on the Midland line from Manchester to St. Pancras and for other cross-country lines. The station had five platforms and a bay. On Bank Holidays some one hundred and eighty trains would pass through Chinley Station. The old Squirrel Inn had been demolished to make way for the Princes Hotel, which was envisaged as a sumptuous staging post for railway travellers, a function it fulfilled fitfully according to the inclinations of the proprietor of the moment. The coming of the railway, and the building of the large station may have caused the people of Chinley to look outwards, but in the first decade of the twentieth century Chinley was an isolated, rural community. Now, all that remains of that extensive station is two through lines, a small prefabricated shelter and a footbridge, and the Princes has become The Squirrel again.

Around and beyond Chinley is an expanse of hills. Immediately to the north is Cracken Edge; to the south Eccles Pike. Beyond them stretch to the north the peat moors of the Dark Peak and a few miles to the south the limestone and green fields of the White Peak, both the essence of Derbyshire. William Simpson is a Derbyshire man. He was born at East Meats Farm (pronounced locally, 'Estmits'), by the hamlet of New Smithy, a mile from Chinley. His mother would arrange 'excursions' up Cracken Edge and Eccles Pike for the younger children in her family during school holidays. William loves the Peak District, and especially the high plateau of Kinder. It is his own miniature Switzerland, a country whose mountains and valleys he says are 'Marvellous!'. (People who knew him will recognise that word. It is said with such relish and is the epitome of his attitude to life.)

Derbyshire plays an important part in his story. Other parts of Northern and Midland England are also very important. But there is none more central to his life than Chinley. He was born there, grew up there, found his vocation there and returned to his beloved Chinley Independent Chapel to live and work in 'retirement'. This church now thrives. It has a good-sized congregation and can look to the future with some confidence, to a great degree thanks to the efforts and inspiration of William Simpson who found it to be on the verge of extinction when he returned to the district to begin retirement in 1965. He became 'temporary' minister, taking very little stipend, other than living in the manse rent free. The intention was to get the church back on its feet and then resume his retirement. He stayed for twelve years.

The Chapel, built in 1711, is the expression of a fiercely independent Dissent. It sprang from the ejection from his living in Glossop in 1662, suffered by Rev. William Bagshawe, who came to be known as the 'Apostle of the Peak'. To have become part of this line of independent congregational ministers begun by William Bagshawe, as he did when he was sixty-seven years old, made William Simpson feel he was blessed indeed. He cherished the memory of the time when, as a boy in his teens, he crept into the pulpit of the Chapel before choir practice 'to see what it was like from up there' and May Birchenough, a member of the choir and a contemporary in age, said, 'You'll be up there proper one day, Willie.' He attended Chinley Chapel as a member of the Sunday School, of the congregation, as Sunday School teacher, as visiting preacher and ultimately as Minister, all his life. Wherever he went to serve in other churches he made it known that at the end of his days he wished to be buried in the graveyard of Chinley Chapel. His Uncle William, after whom he was named, was Sunday School Superintendent for thirty-three years, and you can read the name Simpson on many gravestones. The first Minister to serve in the newly-built chapel in 1711 was the Rev. Dr. James Clegg (William Bagshawe died before the chapel was built). There are Simpsons involved in the history of the chapel from Clegg's time. William Simpson has himself written a brief history of the chapel, 'to the numerous friends of the old place who look back to it as their spiritual home, this little volume is affectionately inscribed by The Author.' Affection for this spiritual home is at the centre of William Simpson's being.

Chinley continues to develop. At one time it was a backwater. It is less so now. A recent erosion of its 'backwater' element has been the by-pass built through the valley in 1987 to take heavy lorries away from the Chapel-en-le-Frith and Whaley Bridge main streets. The new dual highway is half a mile across the valley from Chinley village. The benefit to Chapel and Whaley Bridge is considerable, but it must be at some cost to the peace of Chinley and neighbouring Buxworth. There is a busy factory in Whitehough, next to Chinley, the only access to which for the great lorries is through Chinley village. There is also new housing. People are more prepared now to travel greater distances to work in Manchester, Sheffield and the Potteries. You certainly have to look before you cross the road nowadays in Chinley.

What a contrast, then, with the Chinley of 1900. Then, you could mount a bicycle (with no brakes) at Stubbins Lane and coast down to Green Lane, right to the bottom, ever faster, and be reasonably assured that if you came to grief, it would not be because you hit any other moving traffic. There was no noise of mechanical vehicles. The general peacefulness was punctuated only by the arrivals and departures in the station. Change had come, and more was to come, but in its own measured way. This was the time before the First World War, a war which devastated families, and dramatically began the dismantling of class differences. Before that, people knew their place unequivocally. This is reflected in the housing of those days in Chinley. Factory workers' cottages are at the bottom of the valley. Lower Lane, despite its name, is half way up, and the property there has more space, both within and without. But if you had status or aspirations you went to live in residences on Maynestone Road, which is further up the valley side.

Religious aspirations are somewhat different. Or are they? At the turn of the twentieth century the Established Church would expect its leaders of men, shepherds of the flock, to have breeding, culture and education, and to vote Conservative. The upper social strata would expect their parson to have an outlook compatible with their own, an 'acceptable' pedigree, and to be articulate in their own way. The process leading to qualification as a non-conformist minister would, no doubt, be less constrained. But there were expectations from his own congregations which would be equally difficult to meet. Among these would be an attitude, shown especially by the village folk themselves, which stated that any rough, untutored, local lad should not have any dreams of rising above his station. They would look with suspicion on the upstart who presumed to be different. They could find malicious pleasure in poking fun, and in sneering laughter. And then, to cap it all, the upstart arrived in his first factory workplace with the name of 'Willie'. That was a hazard.

William Simpson knew that they laughed at his calling and at his manner. Far from minding the laughter, he welcomed it. 'If they laugh at you, they've noticed you,' he said. And he was not the slightest bit aware of the social constraints on his aspirations. He did not see life in terms of hazards, barriers and problems. He looked ahead, he saw solutions and there was always hope. After his father died when William Simpson was was only five, his mother was left with nine children, four of them still dependent on her, three still in the early stages of their working life and two established enough to leave home. When Willie was older, in his early teens, he vowed, 'If God sees us through, I shall devote my life to His service.' And then when he was about fourteen years of age an evangelist came to preach at the Wesleyan chapel in Chinley. In Willie's words he was 'God-inspired, a fine personality of wonderful persuasion.' After that, 'my mind never deviated from the idea.' and all the events of his life were, in his own word, 'providential'. He was called and chosen and the Lord put his talents to the most marvellous use.

Chinley School, Summer 1902: Willie Simpson, aged four, fourth from left on third row from back (in infant garb). Brothers Harry and John (second and third from left, respectively) and his half brother Frank Pearson (fifth from left). Sister Lily is seated on front row (fifth child from the right).

2

Early Days

William Simpson was born on 13th June, 1898 at East Meats Farm, Chinley. He was the fourth child to be born to his mother, Annie, but the eighth in the existing family. He soon became known as 'Willie', the name to which he answered throughout his life. Both mother and father had been married before, both widowed. There were four children from his father's previous marriage and one from his mother's.

Willie's mother, Annie, was called Hunter before her first marriage. She came from Donington, a village in Lincolnshire near to Spalding. The landscape around Donington is 'all sky'. The land is flat and exposed to the east wind which comes, at its coldest, from Siberia. In modern times the agriculture has become very largely arable and many hedges have been ripped out to make the land 'economic'. In Annie's childhood potatoes were the basic crop, though animal husbandry was much more significant then than now. Life was very hard and relentlessly bound up in day-to-day survival.

Annie's family had relatives in Worksop in Nottinghamshire. Possibly the connection brought her into domestic service there. It was in Worksop that she met the man who was to be her first husband. He was called Fred Pearson. This man died at the age of twenty-seven, leaving her with one child when she was in her late twenties. She then came to Glossop, some ten miles north of Chinley, to find work as a domestic servant. She lived and worked in Glossop for a short time, and then Zachary Wood Simpson, Willie's father, not long since widowed himself and left with four children to bring up, heard of her and asked her to come and be housekeeper at Dakin's Farm, Chinley, where he was living. They subsequently married, at the parish church at Hope, a village some ten miles to the east of Chinley where Zachary was working at the time. 'She came to him with £50 and a small houseful of furniture,' said Willie. Two children were born to them while they lived at Dakin's Farm, and then they moved to East Meats. Annie and Zachary then sustained their growing family until Zachary's death eleven years later. However, even before his father's death Annie was the major influence on Willie's life and character, his outlook and his faith.

Life expectancy was short, life more precarious in the eighteen-nineties. The family was not cushioned by the state and setbacks were acutely felt. In the face of this Annie had more than the simple, fateful acceptance that characterised so many of her contemporaries. She had drive and determination, a positive will not merely to cope with difficulty, but to use it and surmount it. Drive and determination matter to Willie Simpson. He admires these qualities so much when he sees them in other people. His friend, Sam Longson, a very successful businessman in the transport business in Chapel-en-le-Frith, was renowned for his initiative and application. 'Not many people have the drive and determination of a Longson or a Simpson,' said Willie.

Generations of Simpsons have been farmers and stonemasons. Both callings demand dogged determination. They need the long view, a knowledge of and a respect for the rhythm of the seasons. Out of them comes the economy of experience which lets the elements, the weather or the stone, work for you and with you. Farming and stonemasonry need an eye for detail but also an awareness of the larger design. The product needs patience and time. Zachary Wood Simpson, the sixth of nine children, born to James and Mary Simpson, was a stonemason and a farmer. The farm was a source of food to sustain the family. It was also to provide an income in winter when frost made building work difficult.

Zachary Wood Simpson, Stone Mason, Willie's father.

If you walk about Chinley and Chapel-en-le-Frith you can see a number of examples of Simpson stonemasonry. The indigenous building material of the area is stone, some of it the gritstone of the Dark Peak, some the limestone of the White Peak. There are terraces of houses all over the town which are neat, solid and durable, a metaphor for Willie's life. But for the builder himself of eighty years ago there was a price to pay. The stone had to be cut and there was dust. The stonemason could not expect to live long. Early in life he would be afflicted with 'bronchitis', no doubt exacerbated by the hard Derbyshire winters, which curtailed working life and ensured that few lived to enjoy retirement. The daily work of the stonemason was grinding hard. The building blocks cut for the fronts of houses had to be painstakingly carved and were heavy to manhandle. The stone used for the random walling is awkward and unwieldy. Putting it together is an eternal jigsaw with only the peripheral shape for a pattern. The finished structure is a marvel of achievement. It is no surprise that Willie walked the district and looked with pride and pleasure at the work of his forbears. What he saw, though, betokened more than an achievement of building to him. He saw it is as a monument to the family character.

Within two years of Willie's birth the family moved to Hallgate Farm, less than a mile from East Meats. It was bigger, would have greater potential, and would, no doubt, have been a greater sustainer of the growing family. While they lived there Zachary added an extension to the farmhouse, building in the upper storey an additional little room, chiefly at the bidding of Annie because she could see the day when 'people would want bathrooms upstairs'. Willie always speaks with great admiration for his mother's far-sightedness and her commercial wisdom. In general though, Zachary seems to have over-reached himself in taking on Hallgate Farm. The years of stone dust had taken their toll and his health and strength were declining. By the middle of 1903 they had decided to sell the stock and some of the furnishings and to move elsewhere.

The sale had been set for a Thursday in late October. Two days previously Zachary arrived home from work in distress. His wife had tried to persuade him not to go to work on that day but he had insisted on going because there was a job to finish. His habit was to travel on horseback. Willie, who was five, remembered his father virtually falling off the horse as it brought him into the farmyard. Zachary was taken inside and the doctor summoned. The next morning Annie Simpson woke her children up to tell them that their father had died. He had had a heart attack. Willie remembers little of his father. He does remember him lying on the couch in the sitting room in the afternoon at weekends singing hymns taught in Chinley Chapel Sunday School, resting from a hard week's work. His father 'went to and fro from his work as a stonemason and was always knocking about the farm. He earned two pounds ten shillings a week from his job which was a good wage.' Willie would go with his mother to meet him at Bridgeholme Green, about half a mile from the farm, to ride home on the horse with him. His father was strict, but would only punish the older boys for misdemeanours by sending them to bed without their tea (and mother would slip upstairs with something to eat when father had gone out - a point somewhat out of character in the later image of Annie Simpson). Zachary was a very conscientious workman. He would not leave a job until it was finished. 'Mother often did not know when he was coming home.' (Willie was equally tenacious. The parental model was very powerful even in his tender years.). Willie's only other clear recollection of his father was of sitting between mother and father at the New Year concert in Chinley Chapel Sunday School in the year of his father's death.

The entire family attended his father's funeral in Chinley Chapel. 'I remember exactly where I sat,' said Willie. 'In the widows' pew, which is where the children sit these days.' Even the babe-in-arms, Arthur, was at the funeral, carried by his eldest sister, Alice. (Willie thinks that children of any age should attend funerals. 'It makes them straight up about it all, later in life.')

The sale of stock and family effects was not postponed. There were no telephones and such an occasion was not to be put off lightly. And in any case Annie Simpson was too practical a person not to realise that her family would need feeding. She asked merely that those who bought goods at the sale would wait until after the funeral to collect them. The body lay in the house while the sale was conducted. Willie recalls standing in the school yard at ten minutes to nine on a day soon after the funeral. He saw their dining table, a long, well-made piece which had gone for two pounds ten shillings, a good price, disappearing down the lane on the horse-drawn lorry which belonged to Mr. Ball, the greengrocer from Market Place in Chapel-en-le-Frith. Mrs. Simpson then decided to stay in the house until the next Rent Day, 25th March 1904, a matter of six months, until which date she was entitled to stay. The land was let out to neighbours for winter feeding. There were debts owed to the family, many of which were paid in kind, in foodstuffs, and there was an income from the older children, who were already working. When the family moved from Hallgate Farm, James, the eldest, aged twenty-one, left home to go and live in Gainsborough in Lincolnshire. Alice (eighteen), the next, also left home, to find work in Manchester. Zachariah (sixteen years old) was earning ten shillings a week, John (fourteen years) six shillings and Frank (fourteen) seven shillings. James, Alice, Zachariah and John were the children of Zachary's first marriage. Frank (surnamed Pearson) was the child of Annie's first marriage. The other children were Henry Ernest ('Harry'), aged eleven, Ada Lily ('Lily'), eight years old, William ('Willie'), five, and Arthur, who was four months old.

At the age of forty Annie Simpson was 'bonneted' for the second time (the custom was for the widow to wear a large bonnet with one black ribbon and one white tied under the chin). Four of the sisters in her own large family were all widowed before they were forty years of age. Annie was the only one to remarry. This was the second time that she had been left with a babe in arms. Frank was less than six months old when her first husband had died. There was no ambiguity about her duties to her children. Willie remembered her sitting at the table crying from time to time, but she always ended by throwing her arms up and saying 'There's much to be done!' If you had a family which was totally dependent, then you simply 'got on with it' - a lifetime self-denying ordinance for many an eldest daughter. Apart from that, and of much greater significance, she must have loved her children. You cannot love if you have not been loved and Annie Simpson loved her son, Willie. This gave him his great capacity for love. He loves God, he loves those who were close to him and he loves the people who have been his life as a minister.

Above all Annie Simpson was not a person to allow any situation to dictate to her. She, like her son, Willie, and her daughter, Lily, was always prepared to work and see solutions rather than problems. After Rent Day in March 1904 the family moved to a cottage in Stubbins Lane, Chinley, semi-detached and with just enough room both to accommodate them all and to be a fish and chip shop in the evenings. It had three stories, with the shop on the ground floor and a kitchen behind. There was a living room and a bedroom above that with a further bedroom on the next storey. Then there was an attic. Eight bodies had to be accommodated and, as Willie said, 'There were no space lost.'

Zachary had left an estate of £182, a good sum at the time, but it was left in trust for all the children. He had told Annie that he was going to alter his will so that the money should be used at her discretion, but events overtook them. Annie was advised that a recent change in the law had meant that any money that she could prove she had brought to the marriage could be reclaimed for her immediate needs. She found the executors of the Will helpful. She was able to clothe all the children and send the bill to the executors on the advice of the widow of Willie's Uncle William. Annie's natural assertiveness and resourcefulness kept the family safe in their time of need.

In 1904 Chinley had no place for the young to congregate. So the Simpson fish and chip shop became the focal point for the boys and girls of the village. They would come after six in the evening and then sit on the wall outside and chat. The fish and chips were cooked in a big pan on a coal-fired stove, and all the family were given their jobs to do, fetching water (from a pump down the yard) and coal, preparing food and sustaining a well-run household. At the same time Annie was father and mother to the children. 'We knew her 'No' meant 'No' and her 'Yes' meant 'Yes',' said Willie. She drew lines, life was orderly, everyone was kept occupied and no trouble was brought home. At the same time she encouraged and enabled. When opportunities came in later life for any of the children she was quick to see them and quick to grasp them through her enthusiasm and clear sense of a good thing when she saw it. An example of this was when the chance came, some years later, for Willie's elder brother, Harry, to buy a house. He was hesitant and undecided. Annie had no doubts. When Harry said that he did not have enough money, she said, 'We'll find the money!'

Willie can still see her, 'Walking from this bedroom to that, then to the next one, in her nightdress, getting into bed with us, and saying, "Harry ought to go and buy that house! We can sum up between us." And we summed up and he bought that first house on East View, Chinley. Harry opened it as a little shop. By degrees he brought property here, there and everywhere. He maintained the property with Frank who had become a plumber. House-building is in us.' Annie Simpson knew the value of a proper sharing of family affairs. On many other occasions there were family conferences, generally about finance, around the meal table, usually terminated when Mother said, 'Now you all know. But we must all keep it under the table.'

Having been brought up in the potato-growing districts of Lincolnshire, where a man had 'only fifteen shillings a week' and early potatoes were 'doing well at £21 a ton', Annie Simpson was well versed in thrift and managing. Annie's mother, Mary, was her father, Jeremiah's, second wife. His first wife had died in childbirth, leaving him with four children. As she was dying she told him that he must marry Mary, her sister. He went to Mary and said, 'You've got to come. What can I do with four babies?' They married immediately. She became known to the children as 'the angel mother', such a good soul was she in bringing them up. Annie was the first of ten children she bore to Jeremiah.

Mary and Jeremiah were first cousins. At the time there was a taboo, if not a law, against the marriage of couples so closely related. They had to endure comment from neighbours. 'Here comes old Poll Hunter and all her bastards.' In the face of this they held their heads up high. Confronting unrelenting financial difficulty they kept their heads above water. With this grounding, especially in the position of eldest daughter, it was natural that Annie was to prove such a good parent. She was a religious woman, with a good knowledge of the Bible, quite prepared to pray out loud in any circumstances and with an unshakeable faith. She was quite fearless in speaking out at any gathering. All in all she may appear to have been a dominant, even a domineering personality, who would hold her children in thrall. A strong personality she may have been, but what she sought most was to give her children initiative and drive, to achieve and make out in life. Far from squashing them, they all seem to have taken on her attributes of hard work, an eye always to the future and a keen business sense. They were also well able to make their own choices in life and had the capacity to push projects through to the end. 'What's more,' said Willie, 'she was always cheerful.' When the children became able to look after their mother in her old age they did so with uncomplicated affection, providing the same home comforts and the sense of security which she had given to them.

Willie felt that the business sense and drive which characterised the family were more evident in the children that Annie had given birth to than in her step-children. Either there was an inherited element which Zachary's children did not benefit from or they just did not have Annie's example from an early enough age. She did not reject them. In fact, when James and Alice, the two eldest, left home not long after their father's death she kept close contact with them and gave them help when they asked for it. The fact that they did leave, of course, eased the accommodation problem in the house in Stubbins Lane.

Annie once said to Willie, 'If your father had lived he would have crushed the initiative in the children.' This emanated not from any Victorian cruel dominance on Zachary's part. In fact he appears to have been more indulgent than strict and without any particular drive. She was saying, with characteristic realism, that he would not have fostered independence in the way that she did. Zachary wanted all the boys to be secure in work, apprenticed into a trade if possible, no doubt feeling that his own example was a good one and that he would be securing their future. At the time of his death, James (as a stonemason) and Frank (as a plumber) were apprenticed, and Zachariah and John worked in factories. For her part, Annie wanted to be sure that whatever her children were to do they would do it to the best of their ability. Willie has vivid memories of Annie's sitting by the hearth with Frank with a pot of molten lead practising wiping plumbing joints. If he were to be a plumber, then he was to be the best in Chinley (and beyond).

The family lived on Stubbins Lane for three years. In 1907 a boys' club was due to be opened in Chinley and Annie saw that this would be a counter-attraction to the chip shop as a gathering place. Harry was thirteen by this time and had started work, and the family income was now enough for them to be able to manage without the need to keep a shop. When Mrs. Simpson ceased to trade she left with the respect of the traders and wholesalers who had supplied her. She would stand her corner always, but she was a reliable customer and paid her bills on time. They moved to a two-up, two-down, semi-detached cottage called Meadowbank in Whitehough. Whitehough adjoins Chinley, just across the stream which serviced the Forge bleach works where several of the family were to work.

Meadowbank and the adjoining house have now been made into one. Such changes have altered the character of Whitehough a little and now, of course, people's lives are led differently. The basic physical shape of the hamlet itself remains. Houses have been extended and altered, and new houses have been built in gaps, but the winding course of the road from the valley bottom up to Whitehough Head alters only briefly after it leaves Whitehough, when it takes an uncompromising leap on a new bridge across the new by-pass. In 1907, the road did not have a tarmac surface. It was metalled with limestone chippings, and traffic was almost entirely pedestrian, cycle or by horse. The daily round was concerned with providing and maintaining - providing meals and clothes and maintaining the clothes and the supply of food. Annie Simpson was a good vegetable grower and a resourceful seamstress. The children enjoyed the meals she made. Often she would say, 'Well, I just don't know what we are going to eat today.' But a meal 'fit for Buckingham Palace', as Willie put it, would appear. At Christmas she saved up to have pork and apple sauce. In later years there was to be a goose from Beets Farm. There was always a Christmas pudding, boiled over the fire. Annie's brother would send a hamper from Lincolnshire, an expression of his gratitude for the £25 she had lent him when she was in service. They went for a walk in the afternoon and then had ham salad for tea with home-preserved fruit to follow (Ham Tea was to become a legend in the life of Willie Simpson). After tea there would be a Christmas log on the fire and Mother would read to the family from 'Real Grit' by Silas K. Hocking, O. F. Walton's 'A Peep Behind the Scenes' or 'East Lynne' by Henry Wood.

Annie made all the family's clothes. She bought her material from a draper called Chatterton in Hayfield, some four miles away on the Glossop road. There was not an item they wore that she could not make, from caps to gaiters, and Willie speaks with great pride of the pair of trousers which she made for a cousin out of twenty-two different pieces of cloth. 'And you couldn't see any of the joins, they were so well made and the colours so well blended.' She was never still, her life spent in making or mending. The move from Stubbins Lane must have brought some relief to her with the disappearance of her obligations to the chip chop. She liked reading aloud and would read from the Bible and from a 'good book' like 'Jane Eyre' or 'Great Expectations' to her family every day. Nearby was the Primitive Methodist Chapel where she was a Sunday School teacher. Saturday evening was given to preparing Sunday's lessons.

While they had lived at Stubbins Lane, the children had attended the Sunday School at Chinley Chapel, which was a little over a mile away. The move to Whitehough added nearly half a mile to the walk (unless you were to walk across fields) and so Mrs. Simpson told the children that they should attend the chapel in Whitehough. 'But tell me when you want to go back to Chinley Chapel.' Willie returned within two years, the only break in his connection with the chapel until he left the district to go to college in Nottingham to study for the ministry when he was twenty-three. Chinley Chapel had a special place in the family's heart. One by one all the children returned

'Was there much laughter at home when you were a boy?' Willie does not remember much. Life was serious, there was always plenty to do, but it was a very happy home and the family was bright and optimistic. Later on in life if you were to meet any one of the family and ask how they were, the reply would always be , 'I'm very well,' spoken with great gusto. Willie remembers meeting Arthur in the dark when Arthur did not know to whom he was speaking and being struck by the cheeriness of the greeting. Nevertheless it was a very spartan existence. Nobody had any toys, except Arthur, the youngest, who had a wooden horse that cost 'a shilling (or was it eleven pence?)'. (When asked later in life what possessions he had as a boy, Willie looked nonplussed. You did not expect to have possessions.) At Christmas, you were given an apple, an orange, a new penny and 'an iced pig' (either white or pink). The games they played were 'things like hopscotch and rounders, marbles and shuttlecock and battledore.' On Shrove Tuesday you drank 'Spanish juice', which was water with licorice dropped into it and shaken up to give it a 'Spanish' flavour. Willie went to bed at seven - 'because Arthur did' - and he would read, 'usually the book that you got for a prize at Sunday School. Or Mother would read to us and sing hymns. I remember "Jesus, tender shepherd, hear me".' He would be up at six in the morning, when he would read the Bible for half an hour, not from any particular youthful piety, but simply because he was interested and wanted to know what it said. 'Was there any plan in your approach?' 'No, I just started at Genesis, Chapter 1 and read it through.'

The landlord of Meadowbank came one day in 1910 to give notice that he wanted to live in the house himself. Initially this was a great shock. The family was settled and liked the house. There had been no thought of moving. But Annie Simpson, as we know, was not one to be prostrate before calamity.

She learned that a house with a cellar and more space generally, Ivy Cottage, was soon to become vacant. Ivy Cottage was a couple of hundred yards away round the corner in the terrace which is along from what is now the Old Hall Hotel. Annie suggested to the tenants that they could move to the house, in Whitehough, that was occupied by her own landlord. And so, a triangular move was accomplished, and Annie had the satisfaction of walking over Eccles Pike to Tunstead Milton to fetch her own landlord's notice to quit from his landlord. Harry said, 'You can't do that, Mother!' 'Something has to be done with all these young ones needing shelter,' she asserted. And, of course, she did do something. Providence did step in, as Willie said it did throughout his life, but it must be said that providence and the Simpsons always worked well together. It may have been providential that Ivy Cottage was waiting for them, but it needed a nudge from Annie to ease the move. When Willie Simpson prays, he asks for 'courage and strength' - courage to meet the situation and strength to deal with it ('And I always pray with my head up. Then I'm ready to get going as soon as He answers.'). The Lord will not ask you to deal with anything that you cannot manage. The way will be pointed and the resources are within you if you have the faith and strength to use them. Annie Simpson seemed always to have the resources.

Ivy Cottage had the advantage of more space but the general facilities were still primitive by modern standards. Water for general purposes such as washing had to be brought in buckets from the well just across the road. It was kept in a 'dolly tub' outside the back door, the children's job to replenish it. Drinking water came from a spring nearby which trickled so slowly that it took half an hour to fill a bucket. There was an earth closet.

In the Simpson household everybody had a part to play and everything was done very 'economic'. Mother treadled the sewing machine with one foot and rocked the cradle with the other. She taught Arthur to knit, Willie to darn and sew buttons on and Lily to use the sewing machine. They made their own rugs, 'peg' rugs from old materials cut into strips and knotted to pieces of hessian. A new rug would be made for Christmas Eve. 'We would make a design using something like red flannel.' There came the time when Harry insisted that Willie should put new soles on his clogs. It took Willie some time to accomplish the task and for a week he walked about with a 'pair' which had one round-nosed and one square-nosed clog. He had to learn to hammer in the brass nails neatly and evenly around the edge of the sole. 'When they were all in place you looked rich.' When Lily began taking piano lessons from Miss Lily Nimmis in Chapel-en-le-Frith ('ten shillings and sixpence a quarter') Willie went along with her and waited outside. Immediately they arrived home Lily gave him the lesson that she had just had, reproducing as closely as possible the manner and words of the teacher. 'Now what is before us? It is William Smallwood's pianoforte tutor book.' The family conferences round the table with the theme 'Economy', would consider 'what we owed, what we wanted, how we were going to get it.' The children always knew what was happening and life was always forward-looking. 'You must always have a goal,' said Mrs. Simpson.

All the Simpson children attended Chinley Day School on Buxton Road some half an hour's walk from Whitehough through Chinley. There were a hundred and four scholars, many of whom came from out-of-the-way places in the surrounding hills. The head teacher always had to have an eye on the weather in winter. High Peak winters can be hard. 'If it were approachin' a bad night' the head teacher would tell George Cooper and the Bennetts from Peep o'Day near to Chinley Head, the Moorcrofts from Hayfield Moor and Sarah Anna Cooper and her sister, Winnie, from the Beet to get off home early.' On the other hand, in summer the children would spend their dinner-hours walking into the hills behind New Smithy, towards Hollowshaw, Dewsnaps, Beets and the Wash, devising circular routes which would bring them back to the school gate just as the bell rang for afternoon school. If you stand above Chinley nowadays and look all round the prospect is grand whatever the season. There are few craggy prominences such as are to be found in North Wales. The High Peak is largely a high plain with fissures, which are the dales of the White Peak, and broad, shallow valleys which are characteristic of the Dark Peak. The hills dominate and assimilate even the new by-pass and the factory-chimneys. From Chinley Head the eye is drawn to Chinley itself, and to the chimney of the Forge Bleach Works, but then the eye rises irresistibly to the cone of Eccles Pike, twelve hundred feet high. Willie Simpson's lifelong love of mountains came from walking these hills and living among them.

At Chinley school there were no school meals. You had always to take sandwiches and 'the lady at Dakin's Farm made us a pint of tea'. There would be cold meat on the bread on Monday, bacon on Tuesday, jam on Wednesday, and so on. The head teacher had a simple discipline. He would cane children regularly for the most trivial of offences. Willie was caned every day 'for turning my head.' He was always well-behaved, and invariably conscientious about his work. He conformed to the school rules rigorously, never speaking out of turn, and did not turn his head in anything but a natural way. Nevertheless, at the age of eleven he was caned regularly for it. He told his brother Frank. Frank met the headmaster in the village and asked, 'Is it true our Willie gets caned every day?' It was true. 'Then it had better stop or else you'll have me to deal with.' It stopped. Willie tells the story of a day when a boy, in desperation, threw an inkwell at this bully. 'He was caught and caned almost until he bled. I always went to school in fear. You sat in the classroom dreading the words, "Come out!" and then, "Go and see Mr. Mellor."

The school suffered from a narrowness of outlook. His Majesty's Inspectors exhorted the managers from time to time to increase the number of teachers and to make improvements in the primitive state of the building - fresh water was not laid on in the school until after 1910 - but met with little response. Either public provision of funds for education was chronically inadequate or the local attitude did not hold it in any real esteem. Maybe it was enough for local people merely to keep body and soul together. Successive inspectors' reports at the time during which Willie was a pupil were very damning of the quality of education provided by Chinley School. In 1906, when Willie was just eight years old, the inspector acknowledged the difficulty of teaching sixty children in one room 'in four different standards'. Such a teaching force was 'barely adequate for the needs of the school' but 'the results are in some respects disappointing. In oral lessons the children are rather stolid. A livelier interest on the part of the children is desirable, especially in Nature Study, Geography and History. Oral expression requires more cultivation.' Things had improved marginally in 1908 - the children were 'more responsive' and showed 'greater interest in their work but a higher standard of attainment is still desirable.' A series of recommendations about the building included a comment about the closet - 'The ashpit to be filled up, and pail system adopted, the pails to be emptied weekly.'

A report at the beginning of 1911, two years after Willie had left, states that the school's 'general condition was as previously reported.' There then follows a wonderful illustration of the distance between two worlds - Chinley Day School's and the inspectors':

'To effect a change in the school it would appear to be necessary to bring home to the children the purpose which their school life is intended to serve. They have not been brought to realise that in school they are provided with opportunities for effort, and that the right use of these opportunities should ensure their progress. It is to be feared that many of these opportunities are looked upon by the children as uncongenial tasks rather than as exercises with provision for unaided effort and for mental development. Attention is therefore of the enforced kind and too seldom the result of interest and earnestness. It should be the work of the head teacher to effect a change in the general attitude of the children towards their school life.'

The style of this comment may betray some self-importance and there is no acknowledgment of the environment in which the pupils were growing up, nor of the particular cast of mind of such 'stolid' children. The simplicity, the poverty, the rural remoteness of some children's homes is certainly not granted. On the other hand, there is a basic enlightenment in the educational aspirations expressed. There was a great gulf between what was provided at Chinley School by means of 'enforced attention' and the 'interest and earnestness' which good educational practice would foster. Willie was to rise above this dramatically, his vocation supplying the essential interest, and his very being, the earnestness.

All these extracts are taken from the school log book of the day. The inspectors' reports are, with one exception, the last quoted, copied verbatim into the log book in the hand of the head teacher, Henry Mellor. How he felt at having to record this catalogue of criticism one can only surmise. Perhaps there is some indication by the fact that the 1911 report was entered in the log book by another person. Notwithstanding all this adverse comment he survived in the post until his retirement in 1926. There is no record of how the children felt about him, nor of what his own feelings were about them and of what punishments he gave. Willie certainly did not like him, but he said that 'when he came into the class to teach you something on any topic, but especially about arithmetic, it stuck. He had a way of showing you.'

When the time was approaching for him to leave Chinley School, Willie believed that he would go to New Mills, to the Secondary School, two stops down the line on the railway. Then his mother discovered that Whitehough, though adjoining Chinley, was in the neighbouring parish of Chapel-en-le-Frith and that the secondary schools for which he could qualify, one in Buxton, one in Bakewell, were much too distant for the family to afford to send him. So the last year of his school life was spent in walking the mile and a half up the steep climb over Whitehough Head to Chapel-en-le-Frith Elementary School. There is a great panorama to be seen from Whitehough Head, directly opposite Chinley Head. You can see a great bowl with Chinley in the bottom, and Cracken Edge, Chinley Churn, South Head, with Kinder Scout behind, and Brown Knoll from left to right as you face north. For Willie, 'It was a glorious walk every day. We would set off early for school so that we could loiter.' In his nineties, he still catches his breath as he comes on this prospect, reciting the altitude, in exact number of feet, of all the prominences.

The walk to school in Chapel-en-le-Frith in winter may well have detracted from the view. The heating in school was a relatively new central heating system. Nevertheless if you had walked through rain or snow and your woollen clothes were wet, there was no easy place to dry them. If you did not have the oilskins that Annie made sure her children had, your clothes would steam throughout the day. Willie's particular pride were the gaiters that his mother had made. They were a boon in the snow. Having attended the school for only one year his memories were few but a sharp image remaining in his mind was of the children who came to the school from the workhouse, the Elms (which occupied the site which is now a centre for the elderly, Eccles Fold). These children were visited at school by their mothers, whose access to them seems to have been possible only while they were at school, and that only once a month. Willie remembered the families of workhouse children 'sticking together so close that you couldn't get a sliver of paper between them,' and they were always more than ready to defend themselves against the aggressiveness of other children, physical or verbal. Willie recollected making friends with some of these children. His compassion was evident early, and there may well have been an element of 'there but for the grace of God' in his attitude. When his father had died, Samuel Bradbury, an eminently respected trustee of Chinley Chapel, a friend of the family and a man whom Willie revered throughout his life, had tentatively suggested to Annie that one answer to her problems would be to put two of her children in the workhouse for a period. Lily and Willie were the most appropriate. Annie's response was very firm. No child of hers was going to be found in any workhouse. Her dislike and dread of the place was still with her as she approached the end of her life, and she was to live until nearly ninety. She needed assurance from her children that she would not be 'sent anywhere' if she were to become too infirm to manage. She lived in their care and in comfort until she died.

Willie found his year at Chapel school illuminating in another way. Chapel-en-le-Frith was a market town, tiny by present-day standards, but a busy, thriving, populous community and a great contrast with Chinley. He recalled market day especially, when at lunch times he would watch in fearful fascination the cattle being driven through the streets, drawn by the spectacle, the noise, the assault on his senses, but dreading the possibility that at any moment a beast might run amok.

Willie left Chapel School at the age of thirteen to follow sister Lily into the Forge Bleach and Dye Works. Lily, whose job was tying the fringe knots on finished towels, came home one day to say that Mr. Charles Hadfield wanted a boy to work in the parcel room. This was opportune. Willie had a week of holiday after leaving school and then started at six on a Monday morning to learn the job. The hours of work were from 6 a.m. until 5.30 p.m., with half an hour for breakfast and an hour for dinner at midday. On Saturday the factory closed at twelve noon, work having started as usual at six. This meant five and a half hours' work, not counting the half-hour for breakfast. Willie's working week was fifty-five and a half hours. It was very tiring. He would go home for his tea at five-thirty and then go to bed at seven. 'After a month or so, though, you got used to it and didn't feel so tired.' The change from school to works holidays was equally dramatic. School holidays would have been a minimum of ten weeks a year. Now there were twelve days in all. You were given Christmas Day and Boxing Day, Good Friday, Saturday and Easter Monday, the Thursday and Friday of Whit Week and the week (five and a half working days) of annual works' holiday in August. There was no pay for holidays. The change from school to paid work was draconian. At a stroke childhood vanished. There was no concession to adolescence. It was no wonder that Willie found it difficult to grasp the concept of 'teenage', though it must be said that throughout his adult life he loved to witness the liberty that children came to enjoy as the school-leaving age increased.

Willie thought of J. J. Hadfield as 'a very good employer. He paid his men as much as thirty-five to forty shillings a week and treated them well. Charles Hadfield, J. J.'s son (all the Hadfield sons were employed in the business) was a good man to learn from. He taught you the job well.' J. J. Hadfield was renowned for his ability to handle men. He paid them well in the days before trade unions and, in the context of the times, was said to be never afraid to give them privileges, always treating them as human beings and not as machines. He was a committed Congregationalist, a conscientious supporter of his church in New Mills. He had begun as a boy working in a bleachworks and had 'risen from the ranks'. He never forgot this. He used to lay it upon himself to keep his factory yard clean, especially on Saturdays in readiness for Sundays when the people would walk through on their way to church. A company representative came along to ask the way to the office. J. J. Hadfield directed the man, then took off his overall and went round another way to receive him in his role of owner, much to the man's surprise. As a man of the church he took a particular interest in his employee, William Simpson, who was to come as a lay preacher to New Mills, and then to depart for theological college at about the time when Mr. Hadfield died.

The work in the parcel room was spent in putting together bundles of materials, mostly towelling, which had come to the factory for bleaching, and were destined for wholesalers in large centres like Manchester, the capital of the textile trade. A workmate in the room was George Goddard who was to become Lily's husband. The towels were wrapped in brown paper and secured with string. 'It were no light work to be a packer. It were a work on its own.' Apart from an interval during the 1914-18 war when he worked in the Grey Room (dealing with unbleached cloth) Willie was to remain in the parcel room as a packer until he left for college. At the age of more than ninety Willie showed me with pride the essence of his job. He parcelled a pile of newspapers with an economy of action (and string) and a vigour which spoke of his entire life. He liked to put things and people together. His life's work was to help his people be at one with God. He went about his work in a direct way, addressing problems with energy, much in the manner he made up his parcel. He remembered his roots with pride. Having become a minister of the church was not enough in itself to be given respect and honour. The respect and honour came hand in hand with the affection that his people always felt. 'You're one of us, Willie!'

Whitehough and Chinley were small communities. When Willie started at Hadfield's he would certainly not be among strangers. They, for their part, already knew the young lad with the steel-framed spectacles and the far-away look who had come to work with them. His reputation for other-worldliness, his outlook of someone much older than his years and his religious commitment would have undoubtedly gone before him. They were prepared to take a rise. All newcomers, especially the young ones, are fair game. At breakfast time, at first probably for the lack of anything else to do, the women and girls, the majority in the parcel room, would say, 'Give us a sermon, Willie!' Probably he was being baited. He took it at face value as an earnest request and gave them a little talk. 'It was all a marvellous training.' And in time, because he was unaffected by the malice in them, they who came to scoff found they were listening. And much later when he had fulfilled his vocation those who had doubted him most were the first to claim his acquaintance. Willie's perception was that he was honoured and respected for his calling. 'Men and women would raise their hats to me. My mind never deviated from the idea. I can now see how it were a definite project in my life. I never had any doubts but what I'd get in. I just handed myself over.' The simple wooden cross which Willie put above his work bench was to stay on the wall for many years. When the building was demolished some fifty years later to make way for a re-development of the factory, the cross was still there.

'I had no youth,' said Willie. This is stated as a simple fact. No misfortune is bemoaned, no regrets expressed. He mentioned it from two points of view. The first was that the hours of the day and the days of the week were so occupied that there was no time for play. When he came home from work, even when he had grown enough in physical strength not to feel the tiredness, there was always work to be done to help the family and there was always the work to be done for his vocation, the reading. The second point of view was that his attitude and bearing from an early age were adult, with no adolescent preoccupations. There were those who found this strange, difficult, and who felt he was in pursuit of the unattainable. Mrs. Simpson, on the other hand, quietly accepted her son's mission, making not the slightest noise about it. Her family's achievements would speak for themselves.

Monday morning to Saturday dinner-time was given to work, paid work.

When Willie started at Hadfield's, his pay was seven shillings a week. His brother, Zachariah, got married just as Willie started work and so Willie's little wage did something to soften the blow of the loss of Zack's income. Of the seven shillings Willie kept threepence pocket money. He opened a post office savings account after one month and deposited one shilling - not a penny spent. After a year he had saved twelve shillings. After putting away his first shilling, 'I walked home holding the bank book in front of me.' Thrift, the watchword of the Simpson household, had been given its first tangible expression. He wanted to go to college to become a minister and he knew he had to pay for the training without help. He was never to be diverted from this purpose, the worldly expression of a spiritual goal.

If there was a time of recreation in the sense that we should now think of it, it was Saturday afternoon. When the children were younger Mrs. Simpson arranged rambles with picnics. As Willie became older he went walking, especially with his bosom friend from Chinley Chapel, Edmund Bradbury. Edmund's family lived at Coldwell Clough on the slopes of Kinder. They had a long connection with the farm. Their name was mentioned in the Domesday Book. Edmund's father was Samuel Bradbury, of Chinley Chapel Trustees. Edmund and Willie walked the quarter of a mile or so from Bridgeholme Green to Chinley Chapel through the fields which came out on Buxton Road opposite the church. They sat side by side in the church, invariably affected by the spirit of the place. Some thirty years later they sat together when Willie was getting married to Ida Mary Thawley and Edmund was best man. As they waited Edmund said, 'You know, Willie, there's never a need to feel afraid when you are in this chapel.'

Saturday afternoon gave way to Sunday and Sunday was spent largely in church attendance. Willie enjoyed his Sundays enormously. There was Sunday School in the morning and in the afternoon, followed by Afternoon Service, and then Evening Service. Willie became organ-blower, sitting at the organist's left hand out of sight behind the curtain. For this he received seven shillings and sixpence a quarter. Needless to say it was never spent. It went straight into the growing pile for a college education. The organist was John Waterhouse, a member of an old Chinley family with a long musical tradition which played an important part in the chapel's music. His grand-daughter, Joan Kirk, kept the tradition going. John Waterhouse was a professional photographer who lived at Bowden Head, a mile or so to the east above the chapel. He was impressed by his young organ-blower. He had never had one so absorbed in what was being played.

When Willie told John Waterhouse that his vocation was to become a minister, John suggested that he should become a Sunday School teacher. So, at the age of sixteen Willie took charge of a class of boys who were generally no more than four years his junior. He was not the first William Simpson to be involved in the Sunday School at Chinley Chapel, his namesake uncle having been superintendent for over thirty years. Having been brought up in the school he was thoroughly familiar with its traditions such as the annual outing. This would be to places like Stamford Park in Ashton-under-Lyne, or to Buxton (as far as Buxton, eight or nine miles away!). Every year the children were on tenterhooks as to whether the school would manage to raise the £8 to pay for the outing - and every year they seemed to achieve it - by a whisker! Willie must have prepared his Sunday School lessons with a singleness of mind which belied his years. One of his former pupils, Cecil Hewitt, remembered the class being something of a handful for Willie, but he was completely undaunted. 'He was a stern and a strict teacher.' Willie believed himself to have had a twenty-year-old's attitude and bearing from early in his teens. Any diffidence in approach was out of the question. His immediate purpose was to pass on the Word to his young charges. His ultimate purpose was to prepare himself to do his life's work in the service of his Saviour.

3

The Family

The influences of our childhood years become only too significantly the 'baggage from the past'. The stability which Annie Simpson made for her family was achieved by the closeness symbolised by the family conferences and 'keeping things under the table'. For Willie this meant that loyalty to the family was everything. It is very difficult for him to recall anything which would portray brothers and sisters in anything but a good light. Inevitably then, loyalty became an important theme in his life, very evident in all his dealings with people, and though he will certainly have felt critical of individuals for their behaviour and belief it is hard to get him to express his disapproval - except in the case of fellow clergy, as will be seen later.

Willie's younger brother, Arthur, was four months old when their father died. He was described by their mother as 'the child of their last love', and from the age of nine months he grew up in the home at Stubbin's Lane. It was a secure and stable home. Willie always thinks of Arthur, who had fragile health, as 'loving and gentle'. His friends remembered him as a sensitive, kind boy with a love of nature, who would carefully bury in marked graves any dead animals he found. Arthur would 'greet everyone he met with a word and a smile.' Willie remembers especially his ability to sit and listen to the 'dry theology of Rev. Shuttleworth's sermons' (Rev. Shuttleworth was a minister of Chinley Chapel in the early years of the century)'. Arthur would then come home and write it all down in great and meaningful detail.' Arthur began work as an errand boy at Burgon's grocers in Chinley when he was thirteen. Soon after starting work, the family was shaken by his death. He came home from work one Monday evening in evident physical distress. In Willie's words, he said, 'I don't want to go out any more. It's a sinful world.' Pneumonia developed quickly and took him a week later. Annie sat up every night with him almost until the end. He died a few minutes after Willie had persuaded her that she must go to bed and rest. She had suspected that Arthur would not recover - possibly an expression of the fatalism of the time, or perhaps an unconscious acknowledgment of the place that Arthur had in the life of the family. When Willie woke her to give her the news she said, 'Has my little lamb gone?'

Annie Simpson felt there was a completeness in Arthur's short life. He was the last child she gave birth to. He had lived his life through the time when the family was struggling its hardest. He was thirteen years and eight months old. Immediately after his death Annie went out to teach her Sunday School class. She would not swerve from her duty and she found solace in doing. Willie still cannot conceal the particular poignancy of Arthur's death at such a tender age. It was a blow to them all.

Arthur died while the family was living at Ivy Cottage. They kept his rocking horse (the one that 'cost eleven pence') until they moved to the house in Green Lane several years later. Annie then decided in her quiet, matter-of-fact way that they would dispense with it. Arthur's memory did not need nurturing artificially and there was always the essential Simpson sense of the future. It was a consistent characteristic of Willie throughout his life that dates and anniversaries, of births, deaths, of great events in the family, good or bad, were remembered on the day. ('It's seventy-two years today since Arthur died, Ellis,' he said to Ellis Barnes, a childhood friend of Arthur.) But they were celebratory markers, not maudlin, not backward-looking. Arthur's life was cut short. Losing him was sharply felt. But there was also gratitude to God for his life, the constructive, optimistic acceptance of life given, life taken and life going on.

Lily, the next child older than Willie, born two years earlier, lived to be eighty. 'She always looked serious,' said Willie. 'It wasn't worry. It was just that she took life and its responsibilities seriously. She were a marvellous woman. She saved money and saw possibility in business. She kept the cart on the wheels.' Business was her forte. Her contemporary, almost to the month, was George Goddard. He and Lily were born on neighbouring farms and grew up side by side. There was a sense of the inevitable about their marriage. As they were about to get married, George's uncle was nearing retirement from a flourishing newsagent's business in Tring in Hertfordshire. He offered to let them run the business. Lily, as her mother would have done, seized the opportunity while George was still pondering. They later inherited the business and made it even more successful, expanding into other premises and finally accumulating capital. 'Nobody could go in her shop without you went out with something,' remarked Willie.

All of Annie Simpson's children (including Willie) had this ability to make money and to make money work. They had habits of thrift, hard work, the eye for an opportunity and the courage always to grasp it. Harry, older than Willie by six years, had most of these qualities (despite the initial need for mother's encouragement). The qualities were relatively slow in developing in Harry but as his confidence grew he was able to expand his interests from clog-making, shoe-making and cobbling into property ownership. He ended his days 'well off'. (Willie pointed out with pride a terrace of four substantial red-brick houses in Newtown, houses which Harry had sold 'for £500 each' - a considerable gain on his original investment.)

Harry had some of the Simpson strength of character and down-to-earth approach to life. He had, besides, a bluffness and outgoing humour not seen so much in the others. Willie admired greatly Harry's ability to watch a skill being performed, once only, and that would be enough for him to be able to master it himself. He watched a cobbler attach a bristle to a 'tatchin' end' and wax it to stitch a boot, a skilful process he accomplished instantly. He then said, 'You know, Mother, our greatest expense is footwear. I could do the repairs.' One day when he was fourteen years old he came home with half a sovereign that he had been given by a man in the locality 'for his kindness and his conscientiousness with the people he met and worked for.' Annie was amazed at such generosity and assumed that there must have been a mistake. Surely the man must have meant to give Harry sixpence, a coin very similar in size to a half-sovereign. Harry was sent back to point out the man's 'error'. The man had not made a mistake. Harry had been given ten whole shillings. So Annie suggested to him that he bought ten-shillings-worth of clog-irons to sell to his work-mates at Welch's at a small profit, charging an additional penny for putting them on the clogs.

Before the First World War Harry moved from Welch's to Hadfield's where he was paid twenty-five shillings a week. When the war 1914-18 War began he volunteered and served in the Sherwood Foresters in France, first as a saddle repairer and then riding motor-bikes and sidecars. He survived the war unscathed. After the war he returned to work at Hadfield's. Then, after Annie had persuaded him to buy the house in East View, he set up as a cobbler. He noticed that the quarrymen at Dove Holes and Peak Dale would split the in-steps of their boots because of a fault in the design. So he produced a boot which would stand up to the rigours of the job. He walked in the worst of High Peak weather the five miles to the quarrymen's houses with sacks full of boots to sell. Subsequently his main occupation in life became the purchase and improvement of a number of houses in the area, in Newtown and Hayfield and district. He came to own a 'fair number' of houses, terraced and semi-detached, which, with his brother, Frank, he worked on to provide better amenities. He then allowed his tenants to buy the house they occupied simply by setting a price and letting them pay him over a period of years, without interest (against legal advice).

After Harry's death Willie took over the collection of debts for the property owed to Harry's estate. Willie was punctilious in ensuring that what was outstanding was duly paid. Any impression that the death of Harry eliminated the obligation to complete the payments was quickly and quietly dispelled. When Harry became well off he would ask Norman Kirk, the coal merchant, to deliver a bag of coal anonymously to pensioners he knew would be in need of fuel at Christmas. When he was in hospital terminally ill he asked Willie to arrange delivery as usual. 'Norman knows who the people are. Just ask him to do it and give you the bill.' Harry married relatively late in life. His wife, widowed from her previous marriage, was poor in health and he spent the last nine years of her life caring for her as a chronic invalid. He did not live for more than two years after her death. Willie recalled his brightness, his cheerfulness, his ability always to say he was 'Fine!', even when they both knew that life for him was far from a bed of roses. Stoicism, denial of the severity of difficulty was a Simpson habit. Other people in Chinley and Chapel remember Harry as 'a spark' and 'at opposite end to Willie', much more a man of the world.

Frank was Willie's half-brother. He was the child of Annie's first marriage, given the name Simpson when she married Zachary. When he joined the army in the First World War he resumed the name of Pearson. Frank was fourteen when Zachary died and had already been apprenticed as a plumber. He remained at home until he went away to war. He joined the Royal Engineers and returned after the war, having been invalided out. He suffered a bullet wound in his knee ('on the last Sunday in May in 1915') which put him into Hope Hospital in Salford for two and a half years. The doctors wanted to amputate his leg but he would not allow it, and though the knee-joint was stiff for the rest of his life (he lived to a good age), he took great pride in his mobility and independence. He was a perfectionist in his plumbing - his mother's encouragement and the practice in wiping joints being one factor. He was renowned locally for his meticulous attention to his work. He would finish a job and then, at the end of the normal working day, return at nine in the evening to make sure that everything was working well. Some years after recovering from his war wounds in hospital, he saw a familiar face on Chinley Station. It was the nurse who had nursed him through his injury in Hope Hospital. She was working in Chapel-en-le-Frith. The ultimate consequence of this chance meeting was marriage, a marriage which produced three children, one of whom, Frank, continued to live in Chinley and with his wife, Betty, gives support to Willie in his old age. Willie goes for Sunday dinner there, before afternoon service at Brierley Green.

John was one of Willie's step brothers. As Willie described him, he was 'a fine, good-looking, young man'. His life very unfortunate, although he lived till he was eighty-three. A child of Zachary's first marriage, he was the same age as Frank and one of the seven children Annie had to sustain when their father died. John was earning only seven shillings a week at the time, certainly not enough to give him any independence, and so he remained at home, going out to work at Hadfield's and working at home with his elder brother, Zachary, and with Frank, in keeping the fish and chip business going. He was the member of the family whom Willie described as 'full of high spirits'. He was 'not bad, but he enjoyed going about and having fun and spending money' - not a typical Simpson. Like Frank and Harry, John went away to war and served in India. The family did not hear from him for a year. When news did come it was to say that John had been sent into the hills to recover from illness. Willie later learned, when John came home, that his company had been stricken by enteric fever. Only one survived - John - but he was so badly affected psychologically that he was to spend the rest of his life in hospital. John was two years old when Annie married his father. He would have no recollection of his own mother and Annie had brought him up as one of her own. She and the family visited him regularly in hospital until his death. He died after a lifetime in hospital in Salisbury in 1969.

Willie was sixteen when the First World War began. Had there ever been the possibility that he would have had to go to war? Three brothers had already gone to serve and Willie was the remaining male breadwinner. He was therefore exempt from call-up. 'I don't know what I should have done if I had had to go. I could not have held a gun. I just think it was another example of providence in my life. And, you know, no one ever mentioned it. It never seemed to cross people's minds.'

The remaining brother to stay at home on the death of his father was Zachariah ('Zack'), who left home to be married in 1911. He did not join the forces on the outbreak of war because he was physically unfit. He worked at the Forge bleachworks all his life in the 'croft' where the bleaching process was carried out. His lungs were affected and he was never really well. He died in 1945 at the age of fifty-eight. 'Had father lived he would have been put to a trade.' He married a local girl, Elizabeth Waterhouse. They had one child, but this child died at the age of ten months. They lived on Green Lane in Chinley, two houses down from where Annie later came to live. Willie remembers him as a 'kind and gentle' man who was married to a lady 'equally kind and gentle'. When Willie recollects brother Zack and his wife it is invariably with great warmth. Zack always treated Annie with great kindness, and his wife ('Lizzie') was 'always ready to give a helping hand. She gave herself to the sick and those in failing health. She was always around to give help after childbirth. She had great instincts for nursing.'

The remaining two children, Alice and James, left home very soon after their father's death. Alice came back to live in Whitehough. She was married and had one child, a niece for Willie whom he was to visit regularly in her old age in hospital in Stockport in his nineties.

James was a stonemason like his father. Eventually he went to Gainsborough in Lincolnshire to marry. There were no children. Willie remembers spending his own twenty-first birthday with James. He was on his way to Cleethorpes on the east coast for a holiday and he stayed with James on both outward and homeward journeys 'I had saved £50 by then and I had set aside £4 to go and see the sea for the first time in my life.' James died at about the age of fifty-four.

As the years were to pass, the Simpsons, like many large families, became scattered over the country but Mother at home in Chinley remained the focal point of the closeness of the family, the symbol of determination to keep loss and adversity at bay, so potent for Willie. There were regular visits by all of them to see her there. She was, for her own part, quite prepared to travel about to see them in their own homes where she was made very welcome.

4

Preparations for College

Samuel Heath, a lay preacher, was the mentor of the Congregational Church at Brierley Green for many years before and after the turn of the century. Brierley Green is a hamlet next to Buxworth, a good mile from Chinley. Willie Simpson regarded Brierley Green church as the 'daughter church' to Chinley Chapel, a good proportion of the money to build it in the 1820's having been raised among the members of the Chinley Chapel congregation. The crucial moral and spiritual support to establish the church came from Rev. Ebenezer Glossop, a minister of Chinley Chapel for fifty years. When the subscription moneys had been gathered in for building the church and schoolroom, there was still £70 needed. Rev. Glossop worked hard to make up this deficit. Remarkably, this church did not have its own minister until Willie 'retired' to it in 1977, having relied on visiting ministers and lay preachers.

Samuel Heath was a coal merchant from Didsbury in Manchester who arranged the supply of lay preachers in the area as president of the Manchester and Salford Lay Preachers Society. From this he developed a special interest in Brierley Green, an interest which sustained the church and kept it going against all odds. Some people who worked at Hadfield's attended Brierley Green. Mr. Heath got to know of the dedicated young man, Willie Simpson, from them. In May 1916, the Primitive Methodists in Brierley Green, whose church was nearby, were holding their anniversary celebrations. They had invited local church leaders to take part with them, as was the custom, and as a result there was a vacancy in the Congregational Church pulpit. This provided Willie Simpson with his first opportunity to take a service. He was not quite eighteen years old. 'My subject was "Thy word is a lamp unto my feet and a light unto my path" - Psalm 119, verse 105.'

'Were you surprised to be asked?'

'No, the girls from Hadfield's were there. News soon gets round, you know.'

'Were you nervous?'

'Not especially. But you must never go into the pulpit without feeling a little tense. Professor Henderson, the principal at college, was later to tell me that if you did, you might as well give up.'

Requests to preach in churches in the district soon followed and he became a regular visitor to Cockyard Mission, by Combs Reservoir. (This was not the Church of England building which readers may know nowadays, but, as Willie called it, 'an evangelical wooden hut which a few stalwarts built and maintained - it was well attended. Mr. Bamford from Chinley was the driving force.'). Willie's round of preaching appointments took him also to Whaley Bridge, Kettleshulme, Peak Forest, Thornsett and to Padfield, next to Glossop. He travelled on foot, by bicycle and by any other means he could - as cheaply as possible. There were Sundays when he would take three services, walking twenty miles to and fro. And they all realised a fee, which, needless to say, went into the 'college' fund. He never preached the same sermon twice in the same place. The little book listing every sermon under the place at which it was preached has lasted throughout his life. Nevertheless, he would not take services which took him away from Chinley Chapel more frequently than on alternate Sundays. He did not like to miss worship in his own beloved church, nor did he like to miss seeing his friend, Edmund Bradbury.

This was wartime. John, Frank and Harry were away in the forces. Arthur died early in 1917, so that there remained only Lily and Willie at home with their mother. Willie's mother had had to have a serious operation, a hysterectomy. The physical demands of living in Ivy Cottage were becoming too great for her. So it was a great relief when the family discovered that one of the row of terraced stone houses on Green Lane ('Fletcher's Brew' as the bottom of the hill was known at the time) was becoming vacant. The houses had been built and were rented by the Kirkham family. 'Mrs. Alfred Kirkham had great affection and esteem for Mother. She made it possible for us to become tenants,' said Willie. It was a smaller house, but the rooms were more airy, and, luxury upon luxury, it had hot and cold running water, gas lighting - and a water closet (but no bath). There was no hesitation in moving - a move which was accomplished within a week of being mooted. This was the last house that Willie was to live in in Chinley until he returned nearly fifty years later.

At this stage there came a further, very significant, guiding light in Willie's path to the ministry, another member of the Waterhouse family. Joseph Waterhouse was very much a local character who had lived and worked in Chinley all his life. He was an operative in Welch's works until he retired at the age of seventy, renowned locally for several things. He was very careful with money and well versed, like the Simpsons, in making money work. While he was doing the 'tenting in' (making sure that bleached cloth had no folded edges before it went into the drying machine), he would be visited by Harry Welch, the boss, to have his brains picked about the stock exchange. His knowledge was legendary. He was remarkably widely read and a sharp observer of the social scene, observations he wrote down in rhythmical, rhyming verse - lightly crafted and resourceful humour. Even an order for coal would be despatched in a piece of doggerel. Most significantly for Willie, he was a lay preacher who travelled far and wide in the Peak, many times on foot on much the same beat as Willie Simpson was to tread. Because of his wide reading his sermons were both rigorously researched and rich in illustration, both literary and from personal experience. There remains a body of his writing, all carefully handwritten in exercise books, with not a jot of space wasted. Two pieces catch the eye especially: one is an account of how to construct and deliver a sermon, a succinct and instructive model for any aspiring preacher. The other is a piece called 'It is the Last Time' which gives an account of a number of 'last times' in his life - visits to churches which became difficult to reach, maybe because of his own advancing years, but sometimes, having put himself out considerably, in bad weather, to get to a remote place, he had been offered little or nothing in the way of refreshment or hospitality. In such cases he was not a very forgiving man. The piece ends with the lines

'And so I said, "I'll stay at home,
And rest myself on Sunday.
I'll sit and dream, and raise some steam
That I may work on Monday.
'The subject of my future health
Demands my close attention;
For I aspire and much desire
To draw the Old Age Pension."'

Willie Simpson felt the influence of Joseph Waterhouse particularly in the advice he was given on reading matter. He recommended Bible concordances and commentaries, books of philosophy and history, novels and books of general interest. He also provided opportunities to preach for the young man. When he had a 'double booking' he would pass one of the invitations to Willie. His encouragement was the most valuable element, but only when he was fully satisfied of the young man's commitment. He gave some unequivocal advice, 'If you can't stop out of the ministry, go in. If you can stop out, then don't go.' Do not have any doubts. Willie did not have any doubts.

He visited the Waterhouse home on Lower Lane and sat in the ingle nook by the fire and listened to and talked with Joseph at great length. Willie had great admiration for the man. He believed that had Joseph lived in a later age he would have attained high office as a lay member of the Methodist movement. To read Joseph Waterhouse's writings is to find perhaps too much of the individualist, the sense of his being very much his own man, for him to have allowed himself to be shackled in any way. Willie certainly remembered him as 'a man with his own idiosyncrasies and eccentricities, not given to worldly pleasures, a man whose whole life was religious work.' Again his writing reveals another side. Accounts of life in the village of Chinley as well as of his own daily and annual doings (on holiday, for example) show him to be more worldly than Willie seems to have suspected. On the other hand it was his strength of purpose, his forthrightness, his instinctive awareness of the significance in such a community, of Willie's vocation which must have made his interest and encouragement invaluable. Many years later, in 1945, he wrote the following letter to Willie, a letter which speaks of their mutual respect and of the ultimate contrast in their lives:

'Dear Reverend Brother,

I am now returning the foolscap which you sent me, and I have inscribed upon it what I generally considered was one of my best sermons. This sermon was delivered in Whaley Bridge Wesleyan Chapel on the second Sunday in the year, 1916, practically thirty years ago, at which time I should be at my best. As I descended from the pulpit a gentleman met me, and he said, 'Bless my life, Mr. Waterhouse, you ought to have been a Parson; I don't know whatever your father was thinking of'; and my answer was, 'Unfortunately my father died when I was nine years old, and there was nothing for it but getting into the mill as soon as possible.' And I never saw any chance of getting out of it. Well you can claim that you went one better than I did because your father was dead and you were forced into the mill, but you finally escaped from it, and all honour to the man who climbs the ladder when others look at the ladder and declare that it is unscaleable. I do not know whether you had greater natural ability than I had, but you had a greater ambition, and that ambition you carried out. I never liked the mill, but I have now had almost twelve years of happy retirement, and unpleasant memories of mill life are now becoming dim, and taking things altogether I might have been much worse off than I am.......
Yours
J. Waterhouse'

Joseph Waterhouse also enjoyed a rapport with Willie's mother, their regard for each other founded in their Christianity. He called on her regularly to enquire after Willie, following Willie's ministry carefully, taking what Willie was pleased to feel as a fatherly interest in him. I suspect that the virtues of thrift and plain speaking were also of importance in Joe's and Annie's mutual regard.

The academic preparation needed to go to college was considerable. Willie had left school at the age of thirteen with a basic elementary education. There was much compensatory reading and instruction to be undertaken. He began attending evening classes first in Chapel-en-le-Frith, then in Whaley Bridge and later in New Mills on two or three evenings a week to learn 'algebra, shorthand, book-keeping and to work on English expression'. The shorthand did not prove as valuable as he hoped. He never developed enough confidence in it to be able to use it for note-taking at college. The evening classes were a large commitment. He attended them for seven years, from the age of fourteen until he was twenty-one. They entailed, for the classes at Whaley Bridge, for example, arriving home after finishing work at half-past five, a three-mile walk, two to three hours of instruction, and then a three-mile walk home.

Joseph Waterhouse had given his own kind of guidance and encouragement for reading, - and pithy advice. Rev. W. D. Edmondson of New Mills Congregational Church, a former student of Paton College, Nottingham, who suggested that Willie went there, gave practical help and instruction in preparation for the college entrance examination. Willie walked the four miles from Whitehough and Chinley 'over the tops' to New Mills on Saturday mornings for Greek lessons. (By this time the working week had been reduced to forty-eight hours. Saturday had become a rest day.) He left at nine, arrived at ten for two hours' instruction, and got home by one, 'refreshed in mind and body.' Rev. Edmondson was an erudite and articulate man, a great contrast with his student. But he must have been very alive to the strength of vocation and purpose in his student for they worked hard to ensure that there was no academic obstacle to the realisation of the vocation.

Tutor and student each had his own eloquence. Edmondson's funeral oration for J. J. Hadfield, quoted verbatim in the local press in the twenties, was a very Victorian piece of prose, carefully crafted, not florid but wordy, a detailed picture of an essentially simple man. Willie's eloquence was (and is) in the expression of his daily ministry, the activity, the simple exchanges with people. His sermons are Bible-based; there is always a text; they have a simple, clear message, they also are carefully crafted and delivered, for the most part, in pulpit tones and the Derbyshire accent ironed out as much as possible. The vernacular will assert itself nevertheless, both intentionally and inadvertently, to good effect. In his dealings with people the limitations of his natural language are evident. He has a store of stock phrases: 'I'm all the better for seeing you, my dear', 'Don't I know you?', 'It's so nice to meet royalty,' but all delivered in the warmest of tones and with an expression of great concern which makes you feel special for the umpteenth time. The eloquence is the whole man.

Preaching had enormous importance for Willie at this stage of his life. The other dimensions of being a minister, particularly the pastoral work, were to develop later in life, initially as a student and then when he assumed the full responsibility of a pastorate. But at this stage the preaching played a vital role in his development. He had, of course, to know his Bible and then to nurture the facility for expounding and illuminating the Word for the sake of his congregations. He does not appear ever to have lacked confidence in confronting a congregation, even at a tender age. He appears to have had clear notions as to the manner in which he delivered his sermons, his models derived from the nineteenth century. He spent many hours in preparation, reading and planning the course and the delivery of the sermon in great detail. 'I had no leisure.' It was written verbatim in his neat, copperplate hand, as it always was to be. I imagine there was an untutored rawness in his preaching when he was a very young man before going to college, but his potential as a minister was fully acknowledged. Remarks were heard in Whaley Bridge, in Fernilee and in other places that this was a man destined for the ministry. A lady from Birkdale in Lancashire told him, 'I think you ought to go into the ministry. I'll send you some particulars.'

His sincerity and the strength of his message were plain to see. The work in putting the sermon together, the variety of experience in different congregations, the range of contact with people not quite his own, all were valuable preparation for the vocation, testing his mettle. He never recalls having felt unequal to the task. Besides, this was a source of income, a means of accumulating the money which would be needed to pay for training when he was to go to college.

5

Paton College

Willie Simpson's life has an irresistible sense of the inevitable. To say that leaving Hadfield's to go to Paton College in Nottingham at the age of twenty-three was to take up his vocation in earnest may suggest that the vocation acquired a new intensity. This was not so. A lifelong, naturally developing devotion was taking the next natural step along the way. That is not to say that there were no pangs of emotion as he boarded the train 'at midday on the first Monday in October' in 1921. In his own words, 'It was a wrench.' He felt some apprehension at the prospect of living in a big city. He was familiar with Manchester to some degree, from visits to Rylands Library on Deansgate and to second-hand bookshops. But these were day excursions ('one and twopence, workman's return from Whaley Bridge, and my sandwiches in my pocket'). He felt sadness at leaving the family that he had been parted from for a full week only once in his life, and this only two months previously. During August, 1921 he suffered a bout of bronchitis, one of the rare occasions in his life when he was to succumb to illness. The long hours of hard work at Hadfield's, 'saving all the money I could', the studying for the college entrance examination, the preparation of sermons and the regular walking of the district to conduct services, both on Sundays and on weekday evenings - all had a due to pay. And even Willie Simpson would feel some anxiety about leaving home and taking this great step. Consequently he became ill, and then a member of the congregation at Whaley Bridge decided that he needed a week's holiday at a Christian holiday home in Whitby in north Yorkshire. 'It set me up. I didn't arrive at college half dead.'

Hadfield's were content to let him work out his time with them until the step to college came, a step which had come to be accepted and acknowledged by all as Willie matured in his faith. The company took an interest. J. J. Hadfield had drive and determination (another Simpson hero), lots of business acumen and had made a lot of money, but he never forgot his roots. There was some pride in the pursuit of such a vocation by a factory hand. It was certainly not a usual happening. However, there was no great noise in the send-off. Willie merely left full-time employment with Hadfield's a week before going to Nottingham, saying his good-byes simply and quietly. He returned on a temporary basis as a student during the summer holidays to help out when staff were short. 'George Watson was very ill. I saw Mr. Charles Hadfield and said to him, " George is ill. What do you say if I come back and work." I worked seven weeks. It paid next term's fees.'

The work in the parcel room at the bleachworks had served its purpose. It provided a steady income which played its part in getting the family on its financial feet. It provided a source of savings to be put by for college fees. It gave him the experience of the daily grind in a factory which helped him to understand the demands suffered by the people in the industrial communities he was to serve. Also, it provided a place to practise a ministry. 'You needed courage in a factory. There's a lot of antipathy. They made a bit of fun. Ladies weren't serious in asking for sermons at first but were after a while. It was the men who were prone to take a rise. I came to be called Master Willie, which I thought were a dignified title. Even young children in the street called me Master Willie.' Perhaps his height was a factor here - he was five feet eight inches tall, which may not be tall by modern standards, but he would be noticeably taller than average in his day. Height and his robust health both contributed to the presence he had. Workmates regarded him as 'different', 'other-worldly', but essentially, he was loved and respected, not only for his vocation, but for the way his life expressed his belief and, no doubt, for the way he took the ragging and scoffing and quietly overcame it. He did give the sermons he was asked for at breakfast-times, but maybe the greatest sermon was in the man himself.

Rev. Edmondson may have been instrumental in the choice of Paton College, but there were other influences which made Willie choose to go there as opposed to any other theological college. Paton, he had learned from other sources, made a point of preparing its students for the practicalities of their ministries. It offered a thorough academic curriculum but there was also great emphasis on the work to be done by a minister with people. This suited Willie's temperament admirably.

On arrival in Nottingham he was billeted less than half a mile from the college in a house where he and three other students lived under the care of a sister and brother. The fees to the college, which were £26 an academic year, included the cost of these 'digs'. It was the practice to ensure that newcomers were housed with at least one fourth year student, and ideally, as a mixture of first, second, third and fourth year students, though this was not always possible - for guidance and support. The other major expense was books, the main source being the second-hand shops of Nottingham which were 'Marvellous!' The opportunity to meet such a need as economically as this was also a source of great satisfaction to Willie. The college was sustained financially by the Congregational Union (as it then was), by contributions from such as the Boot's pharmaceutical company (which is based in Nottingham) and by gifts from former students. Hence it was possible for the student to pay less than the apparent cost of his tuition fees and living expenses.

The routine was one of lectures and seminars in the morning, afternoons either working under the wing of a local minister or left to your own devices, with evenings spent in study. Lectures on Saturday mornings finished at eleven so that the students who were to do their pulpit supply work on Sunday at some distance from Nottingham would have time to get to their destinations. The students covered a wide area and must have been a valuable source of supply for the churches around. One such appointment, in fact on his first Sunday in the college, took Willie to Caistor in Lincolnshire. This entailed travelling by train at one-thirty on Saturday to Lincoln, about thirty miles, then by another train to Moortown and then by bus three miles to Caistor. It was unusual for a new student to take a service in this way so soon after beginning the college course. 'I took it because a fourth year student was indisposed,' said Willie. He stayed with a member of the congregation, 'sleeping in a feather bed warmed with a warming pan', on Saturday night, conducted all the Sunday services, stayed a further night, leaving for college at seven-thirty in the morning to return at midday on Monday. He volunteered for this assignment, among other reasons, so that he could visit his aunt, his mother's sister, who was in hospital in Lincoln. 'It was nice to be able to write to mother and tell her how she was.' The students received payment for this work at the going rate for the individual church. Whatever this was they would keep travelling expenses, ten shillings for themselves ('I thought, "My word, I am well off!"') and the residue would go into a central 'pot' which was shared among them all, even the students who had not, for whatever reason, taken any preaching duties, at the end of term 'to pay the fare home'. This share-out was known among them as 'the dividend'.

The students were each placed with a local minister to learn the practicalities of leading a congregation. In this case, Willie's mentor was Rev. C. H. Hedgman, M. A., B. D. of the Boulevard Congregational Church. He remembers his association with Rev. Hedgman as another example of the way divine providence touched his life. This man, a bachelor in his sixties, showed great enlightenment and kindness to Willie. It was from him that Willie acquired the habit of 'five visits a day', the daily pastoral round. He was, inevitably, a very willing pupil. To go and knock on doors and show a warm interest, and to be made welcome, was certainly no penitential duty to Willie Simpson. When you talk to people who belonged to his former churches about him they always remember, above all else, his involvement in the community.

'He worked so hard'; 'he was always about, visiting and helping.' - with chores, in arranging for help which he could not give himself. So, two afternoons a week were spent in visiting members of Hedgman's church, who for the four years of his attachment to them must have been very well looked after. Some, indeed, related better to the helper than to their own minister.

A man like Willie Simpson who has had to carve out his own education, and had to work to compensate for the lack of opportunity in early years, paradoxically perhaps, has too much admiration for the academic achievements of those to whom academic achievement comes easily. Whenever he speaks of Hedgman, he recalls four factors: the five visits a day, Hedgman's love of travel, his 'bell-like' voice in the pulpit and his degree ('By examination, you know - not honorarily conferred.'). Rev. Hedgman's sermons, like those of T. De Witt Talmage, the American Baptist minister whose published sermons Willie had read, had a wealth of illustration from his travels, in Europe and beyond. His maxim was to try to use only those illustrations which he had directly experienced himself. This made a deep impression on Willie. He has since always tried to keep to the same maxim. Hedgman was not slow to identify the thirst for travel in Willie Simpson. He could see that there was a great deal to be done to take him beyond rural Derbyshire. Willie had stood amazed at his first sight of the expanse of the North Sea, unable to grasp the limitlessness of it all. At the end of Willie's first year at Paton Rev. Hedgman told him, 'I want you to go to London. I'll pay for you. I don't want you to go and just be sitting in digs until you come home. I want you to see as much as you possibly can - the more you can see, the more I shall like it. The money's there for you to enjoy it.' He gave Willie seven pounds and ten shillings for the holiday, enough to pay the rail fare, the 'digs' and for getting about the metropolis for a week. Hedgman even stipulated that he should buy a newspaper daily. Characteristically Willie embarked on a systematic visiting of the bridges, the churches, the palaces, the parks, the special gardens, the galleries, etc., etc., going about by bus ('the best possible way of getting to know where places are'). 'I didn't waste a minute.' He arrived back in Nottingham with three-halfpence. 'I kept a very close watch on everything. It were a marvellous foundation. I came from a little tiny village to the heart of a great city. And C. H. Hedgman gave me a wonderful guidebook.' In each of his subsequent years at Paton Hedgman asked him where he would like to go. Each time he chose London again and, having done a very thorough Simpson job on the capital, felt he had made a proper use of the opportunities. Rev. Hedgman really did awaken in him the urge to look beyond. Subsequent travels took him to the Holy Land, to Europe, Scandinavia and to Canada, much of the travel by sea.

The academic demands of the course at Paton College must have been very great for him. The curriculum was wide-ranging: modern history, Old Testament history, literature, philosophy, psychology, logic, ethics, history, Greek and homiletics. He found the going difficult. He relied on others at first for note-taking in lectures. 'They could take notes much more copious than I could. They were used to pen and ink.' (It is interesting that in his nineties he is still using pen and ink. I recall a time when I had not long known Willie. We went to make some changes to the flower rota on his church notice board. I can still hear the noise of nib scratching paper resounding in an empty church. The bottle of Quink and the pen were the entire contents of his battered old briefcase. Statute still requires that newly weds should use the special indelible ink to sign the marriage register and Willie provides pen and inkpot for the purpose, for him a regular echo of an encounter with a punctilious registrar in London.)

It was a great relief to have a fourth year student near to him, an Irishman, who experienced little difficulty with the course. This man was able to provide the insights and explanations which enabled him to cope. Willie remembers this especially in the context of English expression, grammar and points of style which must have figured much more largely at the time, when the stratifications of society were manifested so much more in accent, dialect and grammatical accuracy. 'Derbyshire talk' must still have been a factor to contend with (one of the strictures was about not placing the preposition at the end of the sentence). He was assiduous about his learning as he was in all things. 'I remember declining and conjugating Greek to the buttoning of my waistcoat.'

Thursday mornings were not easy. This was the time of the homiletics class - instruction and practice in the art of preaching. In turn each of the students was required to prepare and give sermons to the rest of the group and tutors. They were then subjected to a rigorous, systematic, critical analysis by both teachers and peers - a baptism of fire. 'The sermon had to be justified in terms of its exegesis, its plan, composition, delivery, words and phrases, its general estimate, and there was always the question, "For whom was its greatest benefit?" recalls Willie, the list recited in feeling detail. 'And after the critics had offered their comment, their criticism was looked at critically.' After the first such occasion Willie's Irish friend said to him, 'You've had enough. No work tonight. I'm taking you to the pictures.' 'We went to see "The Ten Commandments." You break them and they break you.'

His attitude to the course was the same as had been his attitude to all the obstacles in his life. To begin with, the notion of 'obstacle' he would simply refuse to acknowledge. It was a means of exercising his facility for finding solutions. Then, in this case, as in many others, the solution was found in dogged application and determination. 'It were amazing how one dropped into the work.' The particular talents which were to serve him so well as a minister, of relating to people, of motivating and organising, it was not possible at this stage to use to the full. First he had to have the grounding of his college course. And this he acquired by the utmost conscientiousness in his studies, never wavering from his vision of service to the Lord as the leader of a congregation. On the other hand, he believed that the grounding he had in working at Hadfield's equipped him for the ministry far better than did his years as a student. He felt that the uninterrupted path from school to university, to theological college and then into the ministry fell short of the ideal preparation for any minister. This was the perception of a member of the selection panel for Paton College, a mill-owner, who told Willie, when he learned of the years of working at Hadfield's, 'You'll be working at your ministry long after the others have gone.' Seventy years of continuous service (to date) is a resounding vindication of the view. And yet, despite Willie's experience of factory life and of the poverty of his family, what he saw in the slums of Nottingham, especially during the night, when he accompanied a police inspector, Dr. Henderson's son-in-law, on his tour of duty on one occasion, made an ineradicable impression. He also visited a coal mine in the Nottinghamshire coalfield. The seam was no more than thirty inches high. The memory of this visit, the heat, the dust, the noise and the claustrophobic sense of imminent danger still leaves him speechless in old age. It gave him an understanding which served him well when he became a minister. The college was at pains to ensure that its students were not isolated in an academic ivory tower. Dr. Henderson, the principal of Paton College had instigated these experiences for the students. He felt they 'should know something of the realities of people's lives' as Willie said.

Dr. Henderson called Willie into his office one day. He had noticed that there was little variety in what Willie wore day by day. He said, 'I have noticed that no-one is more careful than you. I wondered if you might like to accept this suit length.' Willie was very grateful and had the cloth made up ('for £2'). He wore it for the first time in sermon class and thereafter kept it specially for Sundays when he went out preaching. Inevitably it was to last him many years.

When Willie arrived at Paton College he had accumulated over £200, the amount he calculated would be enough to see him through college, to pay fees, buy books and meet living and travelling expenses. It is not surprising that by the time he had reached the last year of the course, in 1925, he was able to buy a house in Portland Grove, Chinley, for £225 without any need to borrow, so that his mother could live without obligation to pay rent to anyone for as long as she needed. She lived there for over twenty-five years. The habits of frugal living, relatively easy to sustain when you are fully occupied with your vocation, had their rewards. He did not think of what he had done as an act of any special generosity. He was simply meeting a need and providing for the future of the person who had instinctively looked so well to his own future. At the same time as Willie bought the house for his mother's use, Harry bought another house in Portland Grove and Frank a further two, thereby creating a small Simpson enclave in Chinley. Harry, still a bachelor, was living at home with his mother and gave her a generous housekeeping allowance. 'Two pounds when fifteen shillings would have been enough,' recalled Willie. 'She was able to save from it.' (Of course she would be able to save!). Lily assumed the responsibility for paying for heating and lighting for her mother. So Annie was to be able to continue her days with an assured sense of a roof over her head, of food and warmth - a home for all her days. The roof over the head is of great symbolic value to Willie. When he hears of how mortgage arrears deprive people of their homes he shakes a perplexed head at what he believes to be misplaced priorities. 'I can't understand people allowing their rent to go in arrears. You can survive on bread and water but you can't live without a roof over your head.'

It was the practice at Paton to arrange a three-month student-pastorate in a church at the end of the third year of the course. Two students were sent consecutively to preach, so that the congregation would be able to have a view of its candidates. A member of the college committee was a minister in Doncaster in south Yorkshire. He was aware of the needs of the Congregational Church in Mexborough, nearby on the road to Rotherham and Sheffield. This was a mining community about to suffer great hardship in the approaching General Strike. He suggested that Willie and another student should go there and preach with a view to undertaking the student-pastorate. Willie felt at home in this working-class community immediately and took the Sunday services with enthusiasm and vigour, greeting the church-goers as they arrived at the church-door, 'which was unusual', volunteering to help with the Sunday School, which was not expected, and taking a keen interest in the town. The other student did not show the same energetic involvement. So, for three months, Mexborough Congregational Church, which had just lost its Minister, had a young, energetic student pastor. He felt a special affinity with the young people in the church and was able to organise walks and 'excursions' into the surrounding countryside. The new student pastor was greeted by a church member with, 'It's a tough place, this.' Willie's response was, 'If you're young, you're enthusiastic. If you're old, you've experience. I think the first is best in this case.' The student-pastorate must have been very successful because while Willie had gone to London in August on another 'Hedgman excursion', towards the end of the three months, the deacons of the church met and decided to give him the call to become their full-time pastor when he finished his college course. In September, 1924 Dr. Henderson wrote this letter to Willie:

'Dear Mr. Simpson,

I have had two very gratifying letters from Mexbro, one from the Secretary who tells of the splendid work you have done and the new life that has infused into the church, the other from Mr. Gibson saying they are prepared to give you a call. I enclose Mr. Gibson's letter so that you may consider it with your people. My own opinion is that you should consider the offer favourably. So hearty an invitation cannot be lightly turned down. There is no need to come to a decision before you return to college. I shall then communicate with Mr. Gibson.

I heartily congratulate you on the success of your work at Mexbro. The fact that the call was given after a lengthy experience of your ministry shows that the appeal to you is very strong.

With all good wishes,
Yours sincerely,
A. R. Henderson'

The culmination of the student's course at Paton College was the Valedictory Day, the equivalent of a Degree Day. Certificates and prizes were given out. Willie did not receive a prize but his certificate spoke of his being a very good student and of four years fulfilled. He looked back on his time there with great satisfaction.

It had broadened his experience crucially in a number of ways. He had tasted the pleasures of an academic challenge (and success). He had come into contact with people from other corners of society and shared the same challenges. He had undergone specific, and enlightened, training for his vocation. He had heard before going to Paton that it prided itself in turning out working ministers rather than mere academics, a very important factor in his choosing to go there (and no doubt in Paton's acceptance of him). Above all, his abiding memory was of the influence, the encouragement and the help of C. H. Hedgman. 'That man's principles are mine today.' He remembers that at the age of twenty-seven he was described as having the outlook of a man of thirty-seven, a remark he took as a compliment. He certainly had energy and enthusiasm and the same sense of forward looking that he has had since childhood and which has been maintained all his life. 'I'm miserable if I take

A student group at Paton College, Willie (back row extreme left).

it easy. I like to know what I'm doing tomorrow. George V was so right when he said, "Do what you like doing and like what you have to do".' There was certainly plenty to be done in Mexborough.

6

Mexborough Congregational Church in Willie's time, 1925-1935.

MEXBOROUGH

It was the younger members of Mexborough Congregational Church who pressed hardest for William Simpson to be given the call to the pastorate. When he arrived in their midst he showed resourcefulness, organisational flair and an ability to identify with the young members of the church which endeared him immediately. What must have recommended him most was that he was far from being merely a 'Sunday' man. Mexborough was an industrial community, the focus coal-mining and glass-making, but it was surrounded by good countryside, rolling agricultural land with space to ramble and places of historical interest to aim for. The student pastor soon had the young church members who were shop-workers out on rambles on Thursday afternoons, their early-closing day. The members who were miners he took out on Saturday afternoons, their half day. They went to Sprotborough, to Huber (Huber Stand was a great monument from the eighteenth century) and other places, all places of beauty or some special interest reached by a good walk in the open countryside. 'Recreation which would not cost much,' said Willie. No doubt they soon became charmed by the Simpson optimism and zest, not what was expected of the more dour members of his profession they were used to. They would take a bite to eat and a jug with some tea. The only expense for the afternoon would be twopence-halfpenny for hot water - economical pleasure! But how do we stir the jug of tea? The only thing to hand was a walking stick. So 'walking-stick tea' entered the lore of Mexborough Congregational Church, still remembered some sixty-five years later by the remaining 'young' people.

The Deacons of the church met at the end of September 1924. Letters, sent to Dr. Henderson, the Principal of Paton College, and from him to the Deacons, were read out, 'both bearing on the happy results of Mr. Simpson's tenure of the student pastorate'. The minutes then go on to record, 'After carefully discussing the question, the Deacons decided to recommend the church members to extend a call to Mr. William Simpson to become pastor of the church on the termination of his college course in June 1925, at a salary of £225 per annum. The secretary stated that Mr. Simpson would be prepared to accept the above terms.' At the subsequent Church Meeting, in early October, the proposal to give the call to Mr. Simpson was carried unanimously. During the final year of his college course Willie kept in close touch with his church, preaching regularly and presiding over a Special Church Meeting in April 1925 as Pastor-Elect.

In May, 1925 the following letter was received in Mexborough:

'From the Congregational Church at Chinley to the Congregational Church at Mexborough.

Dear Friends,

We hereby transfer to your fellowship our good brother, Mr. William Simpson, who will shortly be coming among you as your pastor.

It is a matter of sincere pride and gratitude to us that a young man who has spent all his early years in our midst, has been called to the great work of the Christian ministry.

Mr. Simpson bears an excellent character and is beloved by all of us. We shall follow his career with deep interest and affection. We have great confidence in him and we believe that with the blessing of God and with the wholehearted sympathy and prayerful support of the members of your church, much good work will be accomplished.

Wishing you and your minister every blessing,
We are yours in Christ's service,
D. Joseph Price, Pastor
John Mellor, Secretary.

A. J. P. Taylor writes of industrial England in the twenties

'The unemployed miner or cotton worker, previously the aristocrat of labour, had a decent, though old-fashioned, house in a reasonably well-kept town. He belonged to a community with a flourishing life and strong loyalties. He paid trade union dues for years, had an account at the local co-operative store. He sang in the Methodist or Baptist choir. Though unemployed he received 'the dole', which enabled him and his family to keep alive. He had been promised recovery and he waited for it (often a very long time).'*

Such was Mexborough when Willie Simpson took up the pastorate.

The Mexborough and Swinton Times of the 11th July, 1925 announces the ordination on the 9th July of Rev. W. Simpson. The service was held in the afternoon and there was a reception in the evening. 'The following were present: The Rev. Moderator E. Johnson Sexton, the Presiding Minister, the Rev. Principal A. R. Henderson, M. A., D. D. [of Paton College], the Rev. Professor H. F. Sanders, B. A., D. D.,Chairman of the Nottingham Congregational Union, the Rev. W. D. Edmondson, Minister at New Mills, and the Rev. D. J. Price, Minister at Chinley.

Mr. D. M. Sinclair (the church secretary) said, "If Mr. Simpson's work among us continues to develop in the same remarkable way that it did during the few months he was with us last year, we shall, ere long be one of the healthiest churches in the country."

'The ordinand, Mr. Simpson, said 'he had reached a great crisis in his life. No new venture was entered upon without some feeling of anxiety, and so his feelings were mixed with joy and sorrow. At the age of five he had entered a Sunday School at Chinley and, up to four years ago had been associated with that Sunday School. He owed a great deal to the Sunday School and to those who taught him and helped to mould his character. He was a member of Chinley Chapel and had continued his membership until he came to Mexborough. When he was invited to become minister at Mexborough he had no hesitation in accepting the call. He believed he could count on their prayers and loyal co-operation in the future.'

*Taylor, A. J. P., 'English History 1914-45' (Oxford, 1963)

A visit to Mexborough nowadays betrays some residue of the past. Physically there are great changes. Towards the end of the twentieth century the town looks to be in a state of chronic redevelopment. A relief road has been laid down, dual carriageway, surgically splitting the town, and taking up almost as much ground as the centre of the town itself. Traffic speeds by, scarcely acknowledging the existence of a community which sits on the edge of the Sheffield-Rotherham conurbation. Its separate identity, as with all such communities has disappeared like all the elements in a Sheffield smelt. There are stretches of green on the road from Sheffield, notably between Rawmarsh and Swinton, but the lasting impression is of a long trail of suburbia and light industry. Some of the public provision, such as a swimming pool, the like of which would have given Mexborough a more tangible sense of itself seems to have been diverted to Swinton. The people who remembered their town in Willie Simpson's day feel they are now the poor relations.

The middle of Mexborough has been redeveloped. The main street has been 'pedestrianised' with new shops and a large new supermarket. The shops meet the shoppers' basic needs, but in common with all small towns across the country, those shops which provide the more specialist services - furnishing, ironmongery ('You know, we had an ironmonger who always had what you asked for, no matter how much you felt you could beat him,' remarked Willie.), and the like have been subsumed into large businesses, which offer a much more restricted choice, or they have disappeared altogether. As a result the focus for many people is not Mexborough itself, but the larger towns beyond; not an isolated phenomenon in the Britain of the late twentieth century.

The present-day congregation of Mexborough Congregational Church lives, almost entirely, beyond the bounds of the town. They come from Swinton, Wath-upon-Dearne and Conisborough and such places. They come to a church, which, from a first impression on a cold January morning, is very evidently struggling to keep body and soul together. There was no minister and there had been none for many years. The church is part of a group whose 'headquarters' are in Swinton. There are many churches without ministers. This places particular demands on stalwart members, church secretaries like Alan Johnson at Mexborough who take on all kinds of responsibility, ranging from the actual, 'hands-on' maintenance of the fabric of the church to being the 'responsible person' for registration duties, as well as for the conducting of services. Somehow churches in this kind of situation survive and even flourish. Mexborough Congregational Church has a large Sunday School ('we do a lot of baptisms') and so there is hope for the future.

The church is fifty yards on the right, up Garden Street as it rises from the main street. It was built in the 1860's in stone which is now blackened with soot. Garden Street now does not live up to its name. There is a plot of land next to the church given to allotments, but it is largely derelict space which lines the street beyond the church. The closing of the main street to traffic brought a steady stream of cars up Garden Street, part of the one-way circulatory system for traffic in the town. Older pictures of the church show a tower, square in construction, capped by a, not-too-squat spire. This had to be removed because it was unsafe and replacement to restore the balance in the design was, quite understandably, beyond the resources of such a church community. When Willie Simpson first arrived in Mexborough at the station down by the river, it was the spire of the church which drew his attention. From the outside it is the blackness of the stone which is most striking. The church resembles a piece of carved coal which expresses all the gloom and dourness of Victorian churchgoing.

Inside, the church has good proportions. Its shape is a broad rectangle and it has a decor which is predominantly dark varnish, with dark red upholstery and carpet. The dais stretches the full width of the church. Behind is the dominant feature, the organ, centrally placed, with the organist in full view. In front of the organ is the other dominant feature, a substantial table with a substantial chair at it centrally, and others to each side. The sense of a presiding non-conformist minister is very strong. There are lecterns to left and right. All this looks on spacious pews set by a broad central aisle with a balcony at the back which projects to almost a third of the area. There must be room for around three hundred people. The current membership is six, though there are sixty children attending the Sunday School.

'I had a hundred people under forty years of age at Mexborough,' Willie said. 'I used to wish that I could find some old ones. What do you think I wish nowadays?' It is easy to assume that the problems encountered by the present-day church in Mexborough are more acute and different in kind from those of years ago. This is not necessarily so. When Willie Simpson arrived there as a student there were indeed more members. There were fewer distractions than there are now. It was easier for the church to be a focal point for the social life of a community. On the other hand, there was undoubtedly less money about. 'A miner had only eight shillings a shift, and he could not be sure of more than three or four shifts a week,' he said. The minutes of church meetings reveal the same issues as there are today. Much of the concern is with raising money, largely to sustain the fabric of the building itself.

When there is an attempt to engage Willie Simpson in conversation about the architecture of his various churches, it is significant that it is more the part the buildings played in giving him and the people an objective to strive for, which occupies his mind, than the intrinsic beauty, or lack of it, of the structure. (The exception is, of course, Chinley Chapel.) The roof at Mexborough needed repairing, the organ had collapsed, the rubble that was the garden needed clearing. These were the concerns and it was only a very short step in the conversation to a discussion of the people, always the people. In fact, as soon as he arrived in Mexborough as a student pastor the organ did collapse. To him it was another example of providence in his life. This was an Opportunity and an Objective. His first instinct was to get it repaired and silence the doubters and worriers, who saw a mounting debt which could not be settled, with 'the Lord will see us through!' The Lord always did seem to see them through, with a little help from his lieutenant, who knew already of sources he could tap. His technique was to make no direct reference to the need but to 'allow' it to arise in conversation in such a way that the eventual donor would be wondering how on earth one could help best. The debt for the organ repairs, £200, was cleared within three months. 'It were amazing how people sent gifts!' Amazing, indeed! There was a service of rededication of the organ on the second Thursday in August, 1925. An additional service always raises a bit more money.

'Money follows me!' again! There is truth in the assertion, but it did receive a firm tug to make sure it followed in the right direction. One day he conducted a funeral at Fernilee, near to Whaley Bridge, and was being taken home by Joshua Lingard, the owner of the wadding mill at Bridgeholme Green, very near to Chinley Chapel. Mr. Lingard was talking about how parsons were always asking for money for this, money for that, of how it never seemed to end and how he would never be such easy meat for the clergy. Willie said he was sure he could 'get into his pocket.' Then he told him a story of a widow who had been member of his church for many years. She lived in an almshouse in Mexborough. She would sandwich a florin between two pennies for the offertory . 'Then they'll think I'm only puttin' in a penny.' When her husband died she slept in the same bed as the body until the day of the funeral. 'We've always slept together. I don't see as why it should change now.' Willie visited her regularly in her old age and she asked him to promise that he would keep by her till the end. Not long before the end she showed him £150 which she kept under her bed. She wanted to leave it to him. He helped her make a will which gave small amounts to other charities and the bulk of her estate to the church ('We don't want to appear greedy, do we?'). By the end of the journey from Fernilee, no more than ten minutes, Mr. Lingard was saying, putting his hand in his pocket, 'How much do you want?' 'Nothing,' said Willie. 'I just said I could get into your pocket.'

It was important for any minister in Mexborough to be able to 'get inside people's pockets.' Willie was warned by his predecessor's wife before he took up the pastorate that this was a church 'with an open mouth'. She was referring specifically to the building. In 1925 it was nearly sixty years old and it needed all kinds of repair work. 'How did you feel having to undertake such a daunting task? Were you not depressed?' 'Oh, I never felt depressed. I just got on with it. I decided that each year there would be a job to do and that I had to set a time limit as to when it would be paid for. When I left they were £2.12s.6d in hand, but we had done a lot and the church was in good condition. I didn't worry at Mexborough. If it were goin' t'wrong way, I just altered it so it would go t'right way. I were determined it wouldn't beat me.' The answer had all the echoes of Annie Simpson.

He expected that the commitment of the people to the church should be practical as well as spiritual. This is an extract from his letter in the church newsletter of December 1931.

> 'The business sessions [of church meetings] can be devotional and prayerful [and] can be as much a means of grace as can divine service. A good Congregationalist will not miss his right at the business session any more than he will miss worship on Sunday.'

On several occasions he went without pay for two months, and once for three months. The arrears were always made up, but it was very much a hand-to-mouth existence for minister as well as church. His housekeeper one day bought a number of items from the grocer on Willie's behalf 'on tick.' The cupboard was bare and there were a couple of days to go before any pay was due. When he saw the goods he asked how they had been paid for. When she told him that they could be paid for at the end of the week he insisted that they be taken back to the shop. He was quite prepared to live on bread and water, if need be, until there was money to pay.

However, much as he enjoyed the challenge of raising money, doing and achieving, the great joy in the Mexborough ministry came from the feeling that he was among his own people. In his own words, 'I fell in love with the people straight away. I lived among them. I could be exactly like a minister.' The use of the word 'like' is interesting. Was he conscious at that stage that he had not yet earned the right to be a 'proper' minister? Was there a clearly defined, preconceived role of minister in his mind? Both questions suggest that, though there was here a man who was supremely unaffected in his sense of vocation (it was in his bones), in his conception of himself as minister he did see himself occupying a particular place, a position he aspired to and which he would enjoy to the full once he attained it. It must be said though, that while he liked this prospect he was under no illusions about the need to earn the position. His great advantage was that the means of earning this position, by working hard, was something he relished.

It did not matter whether or not the people he encountered attended his church. 'Lots of people in Mexborough never went to church, but at t'bottom of 'em they were right good people.' He was about the town night and day, on foot and on his bicycle ('I never cost my churches a penny in travelling expenses.') He would come to the end of a terraced street and ask the first person he saw, 'Is there anyone very ill down here?' A house would be pointed out and he would pay a call. He offered comfort and prayer. He asked if there were any practical help needed that he could give himself or organise through others. Then he would leave the house with a blessing. No visit is ever concluded without a blessing. If you go to see him in his own house, if he comes to see you, if you give him a lift by car, before you part the hat comes off, your arm or hand are lightly grasped, the grip firming rhythmically to punctuate the pattern of the words, and you are blessed. God is generally asked for 'the affection of good courage' and you leave feeling in a state of grace.

The practical help he offered to families nursing the sick, would often be to arrange a rota of people to sit with the ill person at night in order that the family could get some relief. He generally included himself on the rota, especially on Sunday nights when, for some reason, it was difficult to get people to come. His sister-in-law was a nurse. She had taught him how to lay out a dead person, a skill he had to use frequently. A doctor visited one patient on successive Monday mornings and found the minister there on each occasion. On asking why he was 'always' there the doctor discovered that the minister had been at the bedside all night. The doctor then made his own contribution by arranging for a good meal to be sent round on Monday lunchtime - 'chicken with all the trimmings.'

Willie saw the congregation of young people at Mexborough Congregational Church to be looking for a leader and a support. They had little money. 'Miners always spent up every week. I suppose it was because the length of their lives was so uncertain. But I did teach some of the young boys how to save.' An important task was to organise their pleasures. 'I got them to take me on a choice excursion that they admired.' This developed into the regular weekly rambles and then he returned the compliment by taking them into Derbyshire on train and charabanc excursions to Castleton, Grindleford, Baslow, Ashford-in-the-Water, Matlock, Eyam, Tideswell and Taddington Dale. Then they would generally go home via Chinley where they would visit his mother. One outing took them to see the Bradbury family at Coldwell Clough, by Kinder. It was important to Willie that the people from Mexborough should be able see Samuel Bradbury, 'a saint of God' to Willie.

'It was like a pilgrimage.' He was proud to show them his native county. This would cost them four shillings each, an amount which was saved at threepence a week. Importantly, he felt it showed his young charges what organisation was, what could be achieved through it. This stressed the equal importance of process and product. Having an idea, planning for it, garnering the wherewithal, the actual day out, the process, were every bit as much the pleasure as the ultimate reward, the notion that it had all come to fruition and could be remembered, the product.

Willie then broadened ambitions. He took parties of young men on week-long holidays to Ashford-in-the-Water near to Bakewell. He had met a Mr. and Mrs. Brayshaw 'staunch Quakers, eager to help' at a Free Church Council federal conference. They had a house at Ashford with chalets in the garden which were let out to foreign students. They were willing to give the use of the chalets to Willie and the Mexborough young people, an opportunity he took eagerly. He took twelve young men, aged from sixteen to eighteen for a week. They catered for themselves, taking a good proportion of the food with them. 'It cost them ten shillings each, including travel. Albert Smalley, the coal merchant, took us on his lorry. We went out every day on rambles. We all sang under Mr. Brayshaw's window on the day we left.' There were two such holidays.

He felt it was very important that the Sunday School should thrive. Apart from doing 'missionary work' in the district to find youngsters to come to the school, he felt it to be vital that he should encourage the teachers. His admiration for one teacher tells us a great deal about Willie himself. This teacher was a young man of no more than twenty. His great qualities were his loyalty and genuineness, but his stolidity, his earnestness were much less valued by some of his teacher colleagues. They felt that he did not have the ability and learning to justify his position as a Sunday School teacher. They thought his classes were no more than a steady reading of the Bible with little explanation or illumination. They felt that he should be asked to leave. Much to Willie's approval, the Sunday School secretary pointed out the attendance and punctuality record of the class of the twelve boys the young man led - almost perfect. 'Ask the consumer.' The point was taken and the young man remained.

Much to everyone's surprise this young man offered to 'do a turn' at a church concert. No-one knew what he would offer and people were curious, to say the least, at what this 'dull' person would contribute. Then he stood before them all and recited the whole of Corinthians, Chapter 13, word-perfect 'Though I speak with the tongues of men and angels, and have not charity, I am become as sounding brass, or a tinkling cymbal.' There was no applause, just a stunned silence that this should come from so unexpected a source. 'Though......I have not charity it profiteth me nothing. Charity suffereth long and is kind; charity envieth not; charity vaunteth not itself, is not puffed up.' Did the young man choose his text? Or was he chosen?

Initially Willie lived in lodgings in Makin Street, but after eighteen months he moved into a rented house ('sixteen shillings a week and rates') in Adwick Road. Ultimately he bought a house, 16, Alexandra Road, for which he paid £375. It was large enough to entertain people and to have Christmas parties for the fifteen or so boys who were members of his Sunday School class. He remembers one Christmas time when he had visited a sick woman in a miner's cottage to find her wearing her husband's shirt in bed and with scarcely enough bed covers to keep warm. His mother had given him some old nightdresses ('You never know when you will need these.') and he had some blankets. He left the lady with his own cardigan and sent round the blankets and nightdress. The boys who were helping him protested that he would catch cold. 'The Lord won't let me catch cold,' he answered. When they held their Christmas party he was given a surprise parcel. 'Do you know those boys had summed up and bought me a new cardigan!'

The year after his ordination was 1926, the year of the General Strike. A. J. P. Taylor (ibid.) writes of the settlement after the strike:

'The miners were ruined by their own obstinacy. The owners felt free to impose their own terms (undeterred by the expostulations from Baldwin). The miners were forced back to work after six months by starvation. They had to accept longer hours, lower wages and district agreements. The General Strike failed to help them.'

In a community like Mexborough this was more than debilitating. The task of ministering to it was an enormous challenge. Willie's solution during the strike was to offer the miners something to do. In return for no pay other than a bite to eat and cigarettes, a party of miners (and the minister, in dog-collar and working clothes) put in four thousand and eighty man-hours in restoring the grounds of the church, laying paths, landscaping and planting trees. When the job was finished the trees were planted ceremonially and some twenty-six people persuaded to pay for 'a tree to be planted in memory of a relative or friend'. The Chambers family did not plant a tree. Venny Chambers was a florist and he took it upon himself to decorate the church florally for the service, a task he carried out 'marvellously' and one he did equally marvellously for all the Special Occasions which followed at Mexborough, especially the minister's own anniversary. The day of the Tree Planting Dedication, 7th July, 1927, raised £40. It was combined with the Minister's Second Anniversary Celebration, an anniversary which has been observed almost throughout his ministry. The day was a Thursday, half-day closing.

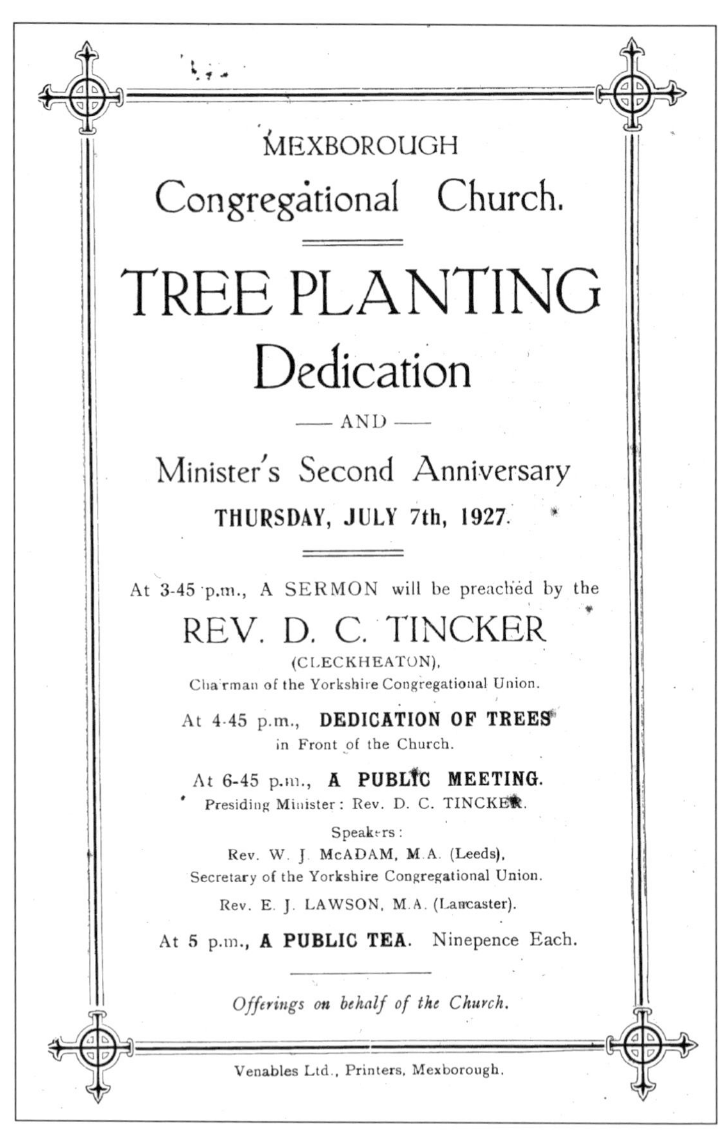
MEXBOROUGH
Congregational Church.

TREE PLANTING
Dedication

— AND —

Minister's Second Anniversary
THURSDAY, JULY 7th, 1927.

At 3-45 p.m., A SERMON will be preached by the
REV. D. C. TINCKER
(CLECKHEATON),
Chairman of the Yorkshire Congregational Union.

At 4-45 p.m., DEDICATION OF TREES
in Front of the Church.

At 6-45 p.m., A PUBLIC MEETING.
Presiding Minister: Rev. D. C. TINCKER.

Speakers:
Rev. W. J. McADAM, M.A. (Leeds),
Secretary of the Yorkshire Congregational Union.
Rev. E. J. LAWSON, M.A. (Lancaster).

At 5 p.m., A PUBLIC TEA. Ninepence Each.

Offerings on behalf of the Church.

Venables Ltd., Printers, Mexborough.

The service began at 3.45, was followed by a dedication ceremony outside the church at 4.45. At 6.45 there was a public meeting. Between the two at five o'clock there was a Public Tea ('Ninepence Each'). All this, with a list of the donors and those in whose memory the trees had been planted, appears in a specially printed order of service - the occasion was given due significance. The idea of the tree-planting ceremony came from Brierley Green. It evoked comment from a minister colleague, 'I wish we'd a dozen Willie Simpsons in Sheffield. I've never know a young man with such organising ideas. The tree-planting ceremony is the idea of a mature minister.'

To help the miners and their families pick up the pieces after the strike for Willie simply meant following his vocation as he had always felt it. He had great admiration for the miner and loved to see him in his pit dirt. 'That meant that he had work and that he and his family had full bellies.' He felt the miner was grossly underpaid. 'His life was hard. When we burn coal we are burning diamonds that men have risked their lives for.' He felt an enormous affection for and identity with the all the folk of the area. 'My Mexborough days were days of great happiness. I used to go out looking for work, not waiting for it.' He believes that God and Christ are to be found all around us in the people we meet. 'Why should we talk of the second coming? Christ has never left us. He came again at Pentecost. He is there before us, in you and in me. I'm not living for some far off event. He's already there! Christ's sacrifices enable us to meet the stern realities of life and through us reveals the glory of the Lord. God has no hands but my hands, no feet but my feet and He can't do His work without the angels and His angels are you and me. And I daresay if we look over our lives we've all been an angel to somebody.'

By way of illustration Willie remembers a time when a member of his congregation at Elsecar church (a church a few miles from Mexborough that he had taken under his wing) had suffered the loss of his wife. This man received the usual formal expressions of condolence from the people around him, but there was one visit which did most to help him. A miner he knew came to his door. In Willie's words, 'It was a man in all his pit dirt, dirty hands and a grimy face. And he said, "Jack, ah couldna go home until ah'd bin to see thee. I canna say owt. But ah know, ah know what it is and what it means. Ah'm thinkin' about thee." That man said it was the finest inspiration he had throughout the whole of his grief. He said it were most wonderful to think that a man should come in that condition to assure him that he were thinkin' about 'im, a man who couldn't write, a man who couldn't say anything, couldn't express his feelings. I felt it was an angel.' The people of Mexborough, who survive to remember those days, recall their own angel who was to be seen about the town on foot and on bicycle, forever raising his hat in greeting to all and sundry. 'We never saw the other parsons about like we saw Mr. Simpson.'

There was a broad weekly routine. The focal point of the week was, of course, Sunday. Mornings in the week were set aside, as far as possible, for the preparation of sermons. Many things could intervene: funerals, emergency calls from the sick and needy, special events, and the like, but the priority was the sermon, and there is now a very large canon of Simpson sermons. On Monday afternoons there was the P.M.A. I first came across this set of initials on reading the church magazine of the period. I couldn't guess what they stood for. When I asked Willie about it there was a slow smile and then a quiet, 'Pleasant Monday Afternoons.' This was a gathering of a group of the more mature lady members of the church, which was, in effect, a service. It was, in Willie's words, 'not a gossiping place'. A talk was given, sometimes by a visiting speaker, and the minister would give 'an epitome of Sunday's sermon.' The session had been in being well before Willie's time and there were those who had been attending for more than forty years. The new minister (who gave it the name, 'P.M.A.') was warned to turn a blind eye if he noticed that some of those present had 'nodded off.' After all, it was Monday, and most present had been up since four in the morning doing the weekly wash. Life was hard and demanding. He remembered especially one occasion when the group held a birthday party for a seventy-year-old lady who had never had a party in her life before. He always wanted the P.M.A. to live up to its name.

Most evenings of the week would be taken up with meetings, of Deacons, of Sunday School teachers, of other groups in the church or of the Free Church Council. Afternoons would be spent on making calls, sustaining the commitment to five visits a day. Every day of the week was occupied. Willie felt very strongly that the minister should be available twenty-four hours a day so long as he was at home. This was relatively easy for him to maintain as a bachelor and even later when married he showed a single-mindedness which many a parson with a family would have found difficult to match. He could not understand any minister who regards his vocation as no more than 'nine to five'. He once telephoned a fellow clergyman to discuss a pastoral matter only to be told by the man that he could not help because he was 'on holiday'. 'How could he be on holiday at home? You are never off duty,' said Willie. No doubt, such a minister, particularly one with a family of children, would feel that his vocation, not to say his family, would both be much better served if the lines were clearly drawn between home and job. Willie's way of getting time off was to go away on holiday once a year, making himself unavailable, recharging his energies and, in the type of holiday which he chose, enriching his knowledge and experience in the service of his ministry. Some eyebrows were raised at his holidays, especially in that he chose to go abroad. But he felt justified and nobody could doubt the strength of his vocation, nor his unrelenting commitment for the rest of the year.

In 1929 he was invited to take part in a Congregational Church mission to Canada, a three-week round trip to what was then a Dominion, which entailed a week at sea in each direction and a week in Canada. At the time the church in Mexborough was in dire need of roof repairs and the members, as usual, had no idea where the money was coming from. There was a meeting on the night before he left for Canada. Willie asserted that he would have the money for the roof by the time he returned. At that time in his life he had a thick mop of fair hair. While on board the ship fellow passengers expressed great admiration for this head of hair. So he said that he would allow himself to be photographed if they would make a contribution towards the roof repairs for his church. The church held a further meeting on the night that he returned from Canada. He had come home with most of the money needed, and enough promised to make up the deficit. The roof repairs were undertaken straight away.

The cost of the mission to Canada, to the most eastern of the provinces, was thirty pounds. Willie was told that there was a source of money derived from a gift by a lady benefactor, which would provide him with twenty pounds. Before he knew of this money he was very hesitant about undertaking the trip and then felt some diffidence about accepting the gift, but members of his church encouraged him to go. It was important to him that he should turn it into an opportunity to meet the needs of his own church.

At about this time an interesting irony arose for Willie. He was invited to visit a church in Poulton-le-Fylde for a weekend to preach. Not long before he was due to make the visit he learned that he was to be the guest in the home of Mr. and Mrs. Harry Mellor, his old headmaster from Chinley and his wife. Mrs. Mellor also taught Willie at Chinley as a supply teacher from time to time ('and was as hard as he was in her own way'). Apparently they had said that they knew him and that they would be pleased to give him accommodation. When Willie arrived by train he got off at one end of the platform and was summoned by a booming voice at the other end, a voice which had for him echoes of childhood, of going to school constantly in fear, and of being caned daily. Nevertheless he found his former head master much mellowed and was persuaded by Mrs. Mellor to stay on a day or two more. She told Willie that her husband was 'a shy man', his big voice being part of his strategy to hide his shyness. This surprised Willie but he accepted it. At least it put this formidable figure of his childhood in a new light and in perspective. Were the Mellors striving to make some reparation? 'While I was there I was treated with such respect, especially by Mrs. Mellor.' They seemed to be very aware of his achievement in rising to the position he was in from beginnings they were well aware of. However, Willie never returned to see them, refusing any subsequent invitations to preach in Poulton.

Willie conducted over six hundred funerals in Mexborough during his ten years there. Life expectancy in those days in such an industrial community, suffering its special hardships, would be considerably less than nowadays. Infant mortality was also a factor. But was a number of six hundred funerals usual under any circumstances? There had been a hint from the members of his former congregation that undertakers would put him in the way of funerals because he would deal with them at short notice. 'Was it an unusually large number?' The answer came with the now familiar slow smile of discovered mischief and in a whisper, 'I used to go looking for them.' In fact, the funerals came his way from a variety of sources. Because he was out in the community so much, he was aware of where all the illness was, and non-churchgoers took him on as their own minister, asking him to officiate when there was loss in the family. There were those which occurred in the natural course of his duties as pastor to his own congregation, and, of course, the undertakers did keep him informed. There was no denying that the funerals were a source of additional income, but there were many instances when the fee ('seven and six for the "top plot", the best ground near to the cemetery gate by the road, four shillings for the bad ground') was either waived because of the family's circumstances, or diverted to another family's needs.

Some members of the congregation expressed a degree of reservation about the people who would come to church for a funeral, especially for those held on Sundays, and for very few other occasions. Willie's response was to say that 'you never knew whether they would come back again or not. It could be years, but there was always the chance that that single experience of church might have sowed a seed.' And, in any case they often contributed something to the upkeep of the church when they came.

'A funeral should not be a sad occasion. It should be faced with a determination to brace, build up and buck up people. There should be something to uplift the people,' Willie says. Given Willie Simpson's brand of Christianity and his optimism this attitude is entirely to be expected. On the other hand, his manner of conducting a funeral is very much of his time. The more grand affairs, such as the funeral of his friend, Sam Longson, renowned in Chapel-en-le-Frith for his success in the haulage business, and in Derby for his chairmanship of Derby County football club, bring out the grand oratorical tones and cadences, with a severe flattening of the Derbyshire accent - until reminiscences of youth occur. Then the accent and the dialect re-assert and the homily becomes homely.

Was there a conscious rationale in Willie Simpson's approach to the office of minister as a young man? Rather, it was almost an unaffected expression of his basic instincts, of what had been instilled from an early age. He believed then, as he still does, in the virtues of hard work, of keeping busy, of providing focal points, of the need for immediate objectives and longer-term aims, achievable goals achieved and the pleasure of working for them shared with family and flock. As he grew in experience, he saw the beneficial effects of the schemes and projects he had undertaken and he began to apply the fruits of his experience in continuing work. But, basically, he followed his own rooted instincts, pursuing a pattern in each of his churches of improving and sustaining self-esteem. The fabric of the church was always important because it was essential that church members should feel self-respect in the place they had set aside for the Lord. They could work together in carrying out the tasks the fabric demanded. They could work together to raise money for professionals to do what was beyond them. They were working together to bestow a legacy on the succeeding generation - another basic strand in Willie's outlook.

Willie Simpson loves a celebration. There is a strong element of the showman in him, an element which, incidentally, contributes to his enjoyment of the pulpit. Celebrations, services specially arranged and constructed like the drama, a joint enterprise for the participants (a very important factor in itself), are held from time to time during the year. He enjoys them so much because they appeal to his love of their special kind of drama. Of equal importance is their function as a focal point. The joy of mutual striving, the satisfaction of mutual achievement are both to be felt in reading the Mexborough Congregational Church Magazine (an organ instituted by Willie Simpson) of the twenties and thirties. There was a Sunday School Anniversary, a Church Anniversary, the Anniversary of the Pastor's Ordination (in 1932 described beforehand as 'a day which will be rich in good things'), special occasions like the Dedication of the Restored Organ and the Tree-Planting Ceremony, as well as all the regular festivals of the Christian Calendar. And, of course, they all raised money.

Important people were called upon to give their patronage to church functions, especially the bazaars, which were held on two consecutive days. The affair would be opened by one dignitary and presided over by two more dignitaries, one for each day. They would be prevailed upon to pay for the compliment they had received. At one bazaar two prints which had been sent by Queen Mary, wife to King George V, were sold. Willie had written to tell her that the church bazaar was taking place. The King and Queen had visited miners in the district after a pit disaster at a nearby mine not long before, while staying at Wentworth with the Fitzwilliam family. Willie reminded Queen Mary of the visit and asked if she would donate a gift to be sold at the bazaar. No-one believed that there would be any response to his request but there was, naturally. How could royalty refuse Willie Simpson? A telegram came wishing the bazaar success and informing of the dispatch of the gifts. The prints were auctioned and one, of a Venetian scene, was bought by the pastor himself as a seventieth birthday present for his mother. Many years later it is still hanging in his home at Buxworth.

Willie Simpson was thoroughly convinced that a ministry should be shared by man and wife. And yet he arrived in Mexborough as a bachelor at the age of twenty-seven and remained so for ten more years. The Mexborough pastorate made great demands on his energy but it was not in his nature to give less than his all. He described a not untypical Sunday thus: 'Morning service, home for dinner, a funeral straight after dinner.' (Funerals were often held on Sundays because they would not then entail time off work for the bereaved.) 'Sunday School at 2 p.m. Then, slip up the steps and across the fields to the cemetery for a funeral at three, then perhaps another at four; evening service, and afterwards the young people would want to go for a walk and would insist that I went with them. I enjoyed it but they didn't know I'd been on my feet all day. I was giving myself all day.' Of course, he could have avoided putting himself in the way of funerals. But in that respect alone he was meeting a real need in the community .

His continuing bachelorhood brought comment. There was speculation, both covert and overt, about possible wives. Willie was very careful not to give encouragement to anyone. He was in the habit of 'going home' to Chinley on a Thursday afternoon about once a month. Each time he returned one of the church members, an older lady, would call in the next morning and say, 'I've called in, Mr. Simpson, to see if you've found a lady.' 'No, Mrs. Bowser, I haven't.' 'Well, the lady you want is under your nose.' But she didn't say who it was.

In fact, the lady under his nose was Ida Mary Thawley, from Swinton. It had taken him a good while to realise it. Whether he noticed her or not until she was brought to his attention is a moot point. As he describes the courtship in his old age he gave no indication to anyone, not even Ida herself, of his attraction to her. And he was categorical in stating that she had never pursued him. So it was, that on the first occasion that he gave any sign of his feelings for her, was when he asked her to be his wife. She was all of fifteen minutes in accepting the proposal. Their subsequent marriage lasted forty-eight years, until Ida's death, a long, contented, joint and mutual service, not without its sorrows, but another example of the intervention of a beneficent providence in the life of Willie Simpson.

Ida was the second of four children, three daughters and a son, of a railway engine driver and his wife. She was thirty years old when Willie proposed to her and was working in the education offices in Swinton. Later, on the day she gave notice of her resignation to get married, she heard of her promotion to a post in Wakefield, a post she never took up. Her family were members of the Congregational Church at Swinton. For some reason Ida had come to Mexborough for her worship several years previously. Willie remembers her family for 'their self-respect and dignity above all else'. Mr. Thawley, Ida's father, Willie recalls, was 'senior, and eminently dependable', in his work, because if there were a special train to be driven, conveying distinguished persons, 'it would be he to whom the honour would be given.' The Thawleys loved their daughters to be well turned out in good quality, tailor-made clothes. In this respect, for Willie, Ida was tailor-made herself. Willie had a very clear notion of the dignity which the wife of any minister should bear. He speaks with reverence of Ida's taste in dress. She wore a hat, customary enough for all women at the time, but she appeared to have revelled in the custom. Coats and dresses and shoes were chosen for their quality and style as much as for practical purpose. Ida was conscious of her status as the minister's wife and came to enjoy living up to it in the manner of her dress. Willie said, 'If she put a rag round her shoulders, she would look nice.'

Among other things, what appealed to Willie in Ida was 'her soundness of character and her ability. She were a cut-out minister's wife.' She worked hard in the church, as a Sunday School teacher, in raising funds, in giving addresses and in the myriad duties a church calls for. The proposal of marriage came one evening when they were in the schoolroom of the church. They were cleaning and tidying up after painting and decorating and had been alone together for an hour or so. Willie suddenly said to her, 'I've been watching you for a long time and I should be pleased to ask if you'd be my wife. You've no need to say now.' Was he nervous? Did he have to gather himself up to speak? 'No,' he replied. 'It just seemed the right time and so I spoke.' Ida's response, almost at once, was that 'she'd given her life to this church and she had worked for it,' and that 'she would gladly accept his offer,' (the vocabulary of which, it must be acknowledged, is very much Willie's). The quickness of her response took Willie by surprise. There must have been an affinity that she was aware of more than he was. They certainly had a great deal in common, coming from similar social backgrounds, and, of course, having a shared faith, not merely a Christian faith, but a particularly accepting, non-judgmental brand of Christianity. As the years were to go by they were to develop to a high degree something they had right at the outset, a facet of some long-lasting relationships between wife and husband. This was the ability to communicate 'invisibly', without word or gesture, the manifestation of a deep-rooted, loving understanding. Never having been able to meet Ida, I cannot say exactly what attraction Willie had for her. Possibly she saw some of her own virtues reflected in Willie, compassion, steadiness, courage. Perhaps she knew that her own quiet quick-wittedness would complement his four-square earnestness. After the proposal they decided to 'keep it quiet' until their engagement, although when they were going on 'an excursion in a charabanc' with a party from the church and they called to collect Ida from her work-place, there were some pointed remarks on how well he seemed to know the way.

They became engaged on Christmas Eve, 1933, when Ida was thirty and Willie thirty-six. Their engagement took place during the service of Holy Communion. The congregation had been given no notice of this addition to the order of service. There was no ring. Before holy communion Ida knelt before Willie and he placed a gold chain and cross around her neck. The concluding paragraph of the pastor's letter in the newsletter for January 1934 says, 'Those present at the morning service on December 24th will long remember the Dedication of Miss I. M. Thawley to the work of the Church. This was followed by the announcement of my engagement to Miss Thawley, after which the Sacrament of the Lord's Supper was observed. Congratulations have been sent by many friends, both far and near, and to all my warmest thanks are extended.'

In Willie's mind this simple ceremony 'lifted her out of the congregation'. Joining him in the ministry gave Ida the opportunity to expand and express her gifts. Together they dedicated their lives in service. Now that they intended to marry he felt it essential that he should take up another pastorate. It would not be right for Ida to remain because 'she would always be Ida Thawley' among the flock. On the other hand, he had no intention of marrying until he knew where he was to move to.

Towards the end of 1934 a student friend from Paton College, Rev. S. F. Townley, asked Willie if he would be best man at his wedding. Rev. Townley had just vacated the pastorate at the Congregational Church at Enderby, a village on the edge of Leicester in the Midlands. This marriage took place in Enderby. While he was there Willie stayed overnight ('in the home of the Page family on Blaby Road') and was invited to preach on the next day. Unknown to Willie the Deacons of the church then met and decided that they had found their man, and subsequently they asked him to come and preach with a view to taking up the pastorate. Willie wrote in the Mexborough newsletter of November, 1934: 'I cannot close my letter to you this month without mentioning the Call which I have received from the Church at Enderby. This Call came unsolicited. At this moment I am giving the matter prayerful consideration. I shall be able to write more fully in the next issue.

My one desire is for your prayers.'

After some consideration the Call was accepted. The letter of his acceptance still exists. It says:

'To the church assembled at Enderby,

After prayerful and careful consideration I am led to the belief that the sphere of service for me is among the people of Enderby.

I am conscious of the high honour you have conferred upon me and the great responsibility that the acceptance of such a call entails. However, I am upheld by the unanimity and heartiness of your decision and the reassurance that I shall have the full and earnest support of all the members. I believe that both the church and myself have been divinely led and that we can rely on God's help and Grace in carrying on the work of the Church. I sincerely trust that the work of the Church may be enriched and prove fruitful for both people and Pastor.

I am looking forward to the New Year when I shall be settled amongst you. My one desire is for your prayers and, in return, I shall remember you daily.

With warmest greetings to you all,

Believe me to remain your sincere friend and Minister Elect,

William Simpson'

The move to Enderby was set for January, 1935. There was now no obstacle to marriage. The day of the wedding was to be 2nd January. The minister's letter of farewell to the congregation in the newsletter of December, 1934 says

My dear Friends,

It is never an easy thing to say farewell. The number of people both of the church and the town who have genuinely expressed their sorrow at my departure, together with their kind wishes for my future Ministry, has been a beautiful reminder that I am leaving many interested friends. ....

My Ministry has not been without its happy hours. I have experienced a multitude of joys in my work. There has been the joy of being able to count on those who have proved faithful even unto the end. Another joy has been that of being able to witness amazing generosity often by members with very meagre means. And what shall I say of the joy of labouring side by side with fellow workers who have toiled uncomplainingly and humbly? Perhaps one of the deepest joys has been of possessing a listening congregation. You have indeed shown a listening ear with regard to pulpit work. Can I possibly omit the joy of being conscious of so many encouraging gestures, such as words and works, that have inspired and helped me from time to time in the course of my Ministry?

So then, these joys have been mine, and I thank God for them because they have meant so much to me............I am not going to forget you, for whilst I shall be adding new friendships I shall always be keenly mindful of old friends. God has mercifully given us a memory so that we may have roses in December..............

It is my parting wish that you will not allow your labours for the church to cease, nor your attendance on Sunday to wane, because there is no regular Ministry. Do not lose heart, but strive to maintain things as normally as possible. This will assist you to secure a successor more easily than if you were to let things get lamentably low.

You will be wise to look after the young folks in the future. Be gracious and large hearted enough not to be jealous of the young holding responsible offices in the various departments of the church. There are churches who would envy you this alone. Enthusiasm has a great claim upon Christian work so I plead with the older friends to support the young. Whatever happens these must not be despised but used. The elder members bring to bear upon Christian work an experience and outlook that youth cannot possibly possess; but it is fatal to neglect the young and to discourage newcomers.

I trust that God will lead you to a right choice of successor, and there will come among you one who will initiate wholehearted enthusiasm, and fill the church with men and women eager to love and serve our Common Master, Jesus Christ. Nothing will delight me more than to hear that the church is becoming a power for good and that the members are rich in good works and Christian example..... '

I remain,

Your sincere Minister and Friend,

William Simpson

It was a small source of disappointment for Willie that his ministry at Mexborough had lasted nine and a half, as opposed to ten, years. Ten years would have rounded it off nicely, apart from making the point emphatically that he would have no truck with the 'fly-by-night' ministries of fewer than five years. All his succeeding ministries were to last twelve years at least. Willie confesses to being 'very tired' at the point of their departure from Mexborough. I believe it was more than simply a physical tiredness. The physical demands were arduous enough, though he was a young man at the height of his energy and enthusiasm following a vocation felt in his very bones, with a wholehearted commitment that he simply did not know how to resist. His robust constitution was an invaluable asset. The joy he felt in his chosen work manifested itself in his good health. The Lord provided the work and the Lord provided the wherewithal.

On the other hand, the person who had told Willie of Mexborough church building's 'open mouth' could well have been talking equally of the town and the people. Willie is still acutely aware of the largeness of spirit of the people in that community and speaks with reverent affection of their directness, their generosity and their simple faith, all inextricably associated with the South Yorkshire dialect (he loves to listen to Irving Gawthrope, a trustee of Chinley Chapel, and a native of South Yorkshire - 'I can hear Mexborough every time he opens his mouth'). But, in the twenties and thirties especially, this was a deprived community. Work for the people was hard and in short supply. The health service was not yet in being and the doctor was called in only at the last resort, often at the pastor's suggestion when he could see plainly that medical help was essential. 'You know, it would cost thirty shillings for the ambulance to take a person to hospital.' The sophisticated, widespread, social provision to be developed after the Second World War was still not in place. Life expectancy was short and it is not surpising that an important element of the minister's farewell letter concerned 'the sick room'. The emotional demands on him must have been very great.

The natural termination of his pastorate, then, came at the right time. Willie remembers every one of his ministries with affection, but Mexborough seems to hold a special place. Maybe he made it his own in a way he did not with the others, until he was to return to Chinley, though each one came to occupy a special place in his heart, nevertheless. All his ministries seemed to come at the right time in his life but the opportunity which Mexborough gave him was the stuff of his dreams. His last service was the Watchnight Service on 31st December 1934. Mr. D. M. Sinclair, the church secretary, presided and 'spoke in highly appreciative terms of the value of Mr. Simpson's ministry not only for Congregationalists but for the whole town.' And now he was to move to a different kind of community in a different area, different, no doubt, as a person because of his exertions in Mexborough, and, most significantly, newly married.

A meeting of the Deacons on 13th November 1934 records the following:
'Mr. Scott proposed, Mr. Smalley seconded:

"That Rev.Simpson, having intimated that he had received a unanimous call from Enderby Congregational Church and having accepted the same, we desire to place on record his faithful service for the past nine and a half years as minister of this church, during which he has worked so energetically for the welfare of the people, and in placing the church in an improved condition and in leaving us without debt. Our prayers are that he may be happy and successful in his new sphere of labour amongst the people of Enderby." Carried.'

Ida and Willie were married in Chinley Chapel by Rev. Dr. A. R. Henderson, the principal of Paton College, an imposing figure, 'six foot six in

Willie and Ida receiving gifts and good wishes at the time of leaving Mexborough, January 1935.

his stockinged feet and everything in proportion, and when he wore a tall hat.....'. It was a tradition that he should conduct the marriage ceremony of his students. The date was 2nd January 1935, the time one p.m., the day a Wednesday. The couple wanted the 1st January but Dr. Henderson was Scottish. The Rev. D. J. Price, the minister of Chinley Chapel, assisted at the service. The Mexborough and Swinton Times reported that 'the service was choral....[and] ... the bride was given away by her father, and was attired in cream and gold silk lace.' There were some twenty people present, largely family. The congregation would surely have been much larger had the ceremony been held in Mexborough, at the bride's home church. However, Chinley Chapel was exerting its influence in Ida's life too. After the ceremony the guests gathered at the home of Frank Pearson, Willie's half brother, in the house which later became a wool shop in the middle of Chinley village. 'We had turkey and all the trimmings and the gentleman who had brought Dr. Henderson by car was kind enough to wait on.' The house was opposite the post office and there was a flow of telegrams across the road punctuating the meal. Among the many presents, letters and cards of congratulation to the newly-weds was this missive from Joseph Waterhouse:

'Dear Reverend Gentleman,

I am sending you a small wedding present, and I am afraid when you first see my gift, so small, and of comparitively small cost; and when moreover you compare it with those costly presents with which you will be inundated, and with those fat cheques of which you will be the recipients, I am afraid that you and your Lady will be inclined to say, 'Well, Mr. Waterhouse might have done better than this, or nothing at all.'

Just wait a minute, my impetuous and hot-blooded young pair of turtle-doves (Remember that Willie was thirty-seven and Ida thirty.) while I have a few words with you on the matter. I think my small present ought to be acceptable for one or two reasons.

1st. It is original. I often read over the lists of wedding presents and often notice how a number of different people have given the same thing - and concerning some things, we only require one and others of the same kind are useless. Though in other cases duplicated articles prove useful by being put by for a time. In old days in this neighbourhood a very popular present was a table-cloth, and it was a very common thing for a newly-married couple to find themselves in possession of as many table cloths as would last them for the duration of their three score years and ten. It is, of course, just possible, but still extremely improbable that any other friend will present you with a copy of 'The Financial Times Investors' Guide'.

2nd. The gift is opportune, coming, as it does, when you are entering the field of Stock Exchange speculation.

3rd. The book contains knowledge which to many people is unusual and highly valuable. Both you and Ida are very well educated and well informed, but this book will introduce you to a field of knowledge hitherto outside your scope and experience. I have looked over its pages and think it most excellent, and if you study it carefully it may save you many financial errors, and by directing your thoughts along right lines it may prove to you not only of present interest but of great eventual profit.

4th. The book is one which will not get out of date. Its information may be as useful many years hence as it is today.

No thanks; we are not wanting to come to the wedding, though we shall listen in if they do have it on the wireless, like that of the Duke and Duchess of Kent. But we thought you would like to take with you to your new home some little memento of the many pleasant talks we have had together on matters social, spiritual and financial.

With sincere wishes for your happiness,
We are, yours
Jos. & S. A. Waterhouse'

(Willie's ventures on to the stock market were to be confined to government securities. Capital which had been accumulated with so much effort was not to be risked wantonly. Simpson thrift and non-conformist blood would not brook too much speculation.)

The honeymoon was two nights at the Sycamores Hotel on the slopes of Eccles Pike, a building still called Sycamores, though no longer an hotel. They then returned to Mexborough where, on the Saturday, Willie conducted a marriage ceremony and after which, having sent furniture on to Enderby, they caught the train to begin a new life in the Midlands. He had been careful to attend properly to his endings in Mexborough. He was to be equally assiduous about his beginnings in Enderby.

7

ENDERBY

The newly-married Simpsons arrived in Enderby late on Saturday afternoon, 5th January 1935. The manse, an early nineteenth-century redbrick house, stone-faced on its southern aspect, with an imposing view southwards from its front windows, was not ready for them to occupy immediately and so they stayed with the Page family until Monday morning when the furniture arrived and they could begin the process of settling in. The extent of the change in Willie's life at this point was considerable. He was in a new pastorate, about to occupy a new home, in a very different community from Mexborough, and most significantly, embarking on married life. The memory of the time is of weariness, from relentless commitment in Mexborough. He also recalls vividly the sense of change. I imagined that the adjustment to change on such a scale would have taken several months, at least. In fact, he said it took 'about a month'.

The Simpsons tackled the situation in a beautifully simple way. They undertook a series of personal calls on all the members of their new church. They walked round the village and the district, knocked on doors and said, 'Hello.' Willie gave notice of the impending visits from the pulpit on Sunday, saying which streets and areas they would be visiting in the coming week. This served a variety of purposes. It gave Willie the sense of really 'doing'. His way of dealing with tiredness and even impending trauma was to be active. It was a tangibly joint venture of minister and wife from the outset. The pastorate would then belong to both of them, not just to him. The people of Enderby, and not just those who came to the Congregational Church, came to know them both at the earliest possible moment and they were able to get a more rounded picture of their new flock in their own homes. They walked the village and the district, becoming familiar with its shape and its feel in the way that only the slow progress on foot can achieve. The Simpsons also invited all the members of the church, according to Mrs. Mary Lowe, 'in fours and sixes to tea on Sunday afternoons on purpose to get to know them.' It did not take long before they were all thoroughly acquainted.

Enderby sits on a knoll. Nowadays, it is in an angle of the junction of two motorways, the M1 and the M69. It is about four miles from the centre of the city of Leicester and is part of the parliamentary constituency of Blaby. Think of Enderby as the centre point of a shallow arc which begins with Blaby and extends through Whetstone and Narborough to Huncote, none of them more than two miles away from Enderby nor more than two miles between villages. As you pass on the M1 or go across the fields towards Huncote across a flat area Enderby stands out. On top of the knoll is a sand-coloured brick church, Enderby United Reformed Church (formerly the Congregational Church), visible all round, and known locally as the 'top church'. It is now recognised by the local council as a landmark worthy of preservation. It was built in 1910, replacing a chapel built, as the manse was, in the early nineeenth century. The old chapel now serves as the church hall, fulfilling the muliplicity of purposes which all such buildings come to meet; for Sunday School, for playgroups, for church meetings, and in pre- and immediately post-war days, for drama and music.

During the war the building resumed its first function as a church when evening service was held there. They could not 'black out' the 'new' church and there was no street lighting after dark. So evening service moved to the old building. The atmosphere that this generated in the old chapel at this time affected Willie deeply. The black-out curtains helped create an intimacy to which the congregation responded, especially the older members who remembered coming to services before the new church was built. Some went to sit in the pews they used to sit in as children when they attended church with their parents. Others went to the seats they used to occupy in the balcony. There was no lectern for the minister to preach from, just a simple dais. So, having nowhere to put his notes, Willie would preach extempore. 'I had enough sermons up my sleeve to manage that.' The occasions must have been very special. The time of war brought people much closer together. These services in the old, hallowed building, a sanctuary in the surrounding darkness, became a palpable expression of the way people were feeling, under threat from the war, uncertain and seeking the closeness and support of neighbours.

The three buildings, the old chapel, the church and the manse, together hold a tightly-knit site, approached uphill from all directions. Enderby Congregational Church contrasts sharply with Mexborough Congregational Church. At the time of the Simpsons' arrival it was a mere twenty-five years old. It must have felt quite new. Today it still has a sense of newness. The design gives it an air of solidity, but there is also a sense of light and space which seem to be lacking from the church at Mexborough, despite the essential spaciousness of the interior there. There is certainly no Victorian oppressive gloom about the Enderby church. It has a feel of the thirties, despite its vintage. It is high-ceilinged, 'too high to be warm' in the words of present-day members, and there's 'too much brass to polish'. The present-day population of Enderby does not give the impression of great prosperity, but there appears to be a smaller sense of struggle in maintaining the church building than is felt in Mexborough. This may well reflect the respective age of the two buildings, and the fact that where the earlier one bears the marks of its place in the grime of industry, the later one has had the benefit of a situation at least semi-rural from its beginnings. In this respect each church reflects its community.

The part of the village of Enderby which immediately surrounds the Congregational Church is the oldest part. There is thatch, and there are Georgian and Victorian brick terraces. Beyond this there is a startling lack of unity in the design of housing, both in the original village and in the surrounding development. There are sixties' houses built in ones, twos, threes and fours here and there, among older Victorian and Edwardian redbrick terraces, with little space left anywhere. There are streets, now paved with 'modern' brick paving and cream-coloured flagstones. There are odd spaces on these streets which have been filled, to the brim, with modern bungalows with paved 'gardens'. There are some unadopted roads whose surface has a studied neglect in contrast with the well-tended bungalows which line them. At one time the Co-operative movement built a shoe factory in Enderby. The movement's influence must have been felt beyond the factory gates. There is an Equity Road, a Co-operation Street, and a Federation Street.

As for most communities the advent of the motor-car and the widening of car ownership has been seminal in the alteration of Enderby. There is a feeling of a halt in the progress of time in the immediate vicinity of the Congregational Church, but beyond there, it looked and felt like a commuter suburb, easily left and easily obtained through the distance-shrinking car. Within Enderby and beyond, across the fields towards Huncote, the hum of traffic was inescapable. On a languid June afternoon the noise of an accelerating motor-cycle did not stand out. In 1935, on the other hand, it was calm and separate from Leicester. Many in the village worked in the shoe factories and hosiery mills there but it was a distant enough four miles to allow the village its own identity.

A local man, Sam Kilby, was an ardent cine enthusiast. He kept a record on film over twenty years, from the thirties to the fifties, of many aspects of the life of Enderby, village and church fetes and gala days, times of flood and snow, and snippets of day-to-day life. Now he has put together a selection from his films on video-tape with his own commentary 'voiced-over' in authentic Leicestershire tones. It provides a revealing insight into the life of the village at the time when Willie Simpson was in his ministry there. There is even a picture of a sprightly, forty-year-old, Rev. Simpson dancing with the children at a church fete. The compilation is a valuable social document, all the more fascinating and revealing for the sepia tones which intervene among the basic black and white and occasional faded colour film. Life was slower then and pleasures had much less sophistication.

Willie's first discovery at Enderby was that there was less for him to do. (Not that he would have revelled in an easier working day. In fact, he soon solved the problem of inactivity by 'making work'.) Whereas he had found that the people of Mexborough needed his ministry, the people of Enderby wanted to minister to him and to Ida. He found this difficult to adjust to. The people were more self-sufficient - there was not the same poverty as he had had to contend with in Mexborough. People talked more easily but were less forthright. You did not know exactly where you stood, as you did in Mexborough, until you became able to read the hidden message. In their early days in Enderby an old lady came to the door of the manse offering advice. 'You're new here. Let me tell you to beware the smooth tongue.' 'You know, she was right. There were those who said nice things, but you could tell how they were by the way they dealt with one another.' Ida's presence was providential in this respect. He spoke with wonder at her ability to size people up. She knew glibness when she saw it. She could identify a dissembler. She was aware of the people they sometimes had to deal with in a way that her husband was not. She was the essential support for him in this new ministry. He would have been very much at sea without her.

Ida's energy seems to have matched Willie's. The manse needed a great deal of work and so they set about renovating, modernising and decorating. They brought about the removal of bedroom fireplaces with oven and boiler which needed black-leading. They covered brick floors with tiles and brightened and cleaned everywhere about the house. 'There was brown and green paint everywhere so that it would not need painting often. My wife liked decorating. So we got to work. It took two years to finish the job.' The cost of the work was a factor. Willie decided that the sources of income which were beyond his stipend (which was the same as at Mexborough - £225 per annum) - fees for funerals, baptisms and marriages, should be put into a fund 'for the Restoration of the Manse'. The practice in the church was for the fee for the minister's services for funerals to be restored to the family when the minister visited after the service. He conducted a funeral for a branch of the Young family ('there were nineteen Young families in Enderby - one half unrelated to the other'). He paid the customary visit to the family, but broke the tradition of restoring the fee and told them of his intention. 'Mr. Young approved wholeheartedly' and made a further contribution immediately to the Restoration Fund. There was plain good sense in the idea. It benefited both church and minister and his wife. Despite marriage and having two mouths to feed instead of one Willie felt better off with the move to Enderby. He no longer had to find his own place to live, nor to pay a housekeeper.

Probably it took Willie longer than 'about a month' to settle in Enderby. It was to be twelve years before he and Ida moved to another church, during which time the Second World War occurred. He undertook to 'see the people at Enderby through the war, however long it was to take', and then when he did move on to a district of Walsall in the Black Country, he was 'glad to have something to get my teeth into.' Both points are revealing of his feelings about Enderby. It gave him the chance to recoup energies spent in Mexborough. It provided the opportunity to practise a ministry among folk not so much his own as those in Mexborough. It was a good start to married life for both of them. But there is a slight sense of self-imposed obligation in the words 'however long it takes', characteristically determined, but untypically lacking full enthusiasm. There was simply not enough physical need for him to meet.

On the other hand, again, the abiding impression of those who remember his ministry is that 'he worked so hard'. The 'five-calls-a-day' rule remained. He would make the calls on foot, if they were nearby. Walking about was not entirely without hazard. Crossing the fields one day to Huncote he was butted by a ram. Perhaps the ram saw a rival for his flock. Further afield he would reach by bicycle. Willie has happy memories of bowling along the Leicestershire lanes to visit his people in their homes or in hospital in Leicester or even further afield. He also took under his wing some of the churches in surrounding villages, those without a minister (at Whetstone, Blaby and Huncote) where he would perform the offices at funerals, baptisms and marriages, as well as conducting occasional Sunday services. Everyone he met would be greeted. He seemed permanently to be cycling one-handed, the other hand forever raising his hat in greeting.

The bicycle was an important part of the Simpson persona. It did have its hazards. One man recalled Willie's coming down High Street, Enderby, a

fairly steep hill, to go across to Leicester Lane and narrowly missing a lorry from the quarry. Ernest Hubbard, who witnessed the incident, said, 'God must have guided him round that vehicle.' But Willie had never considered any other means of transport for getting about his patch. It made a great difference to the scope of his work in the district. It kept him in close touch with the people because of its natural pace. It cost next-to-nothing to run and evoked the familiar refrain, 'I never cost my churches a penny for transport.'- the constant reminder of the parsimony of his childhood. It took him about the district with only as much noise as he would make as a person, and no more - not that it was in his nature to creep by unnoticed. It provided a blend; it facilitated visiting, to more homes and further afield, and it kept all and sundry within hailing distance as he went about. The slow pace and steady rhythm of his comings and goings fostered close contact with his people. This was no cocooning car, tunnel-thread between the two ends of a journey. On the bicycle he was open to the sounds, the smells, the changes, the shifts in the minutiae which happen beyond the motorist's ken. And he was seen to be about. People knew from the evidence of their own eyes that he was among them. His arrival on the bicycle to make a visit would be gentle. It would have an in-built hesitancy, an old-world reticence to temper the essential familiarity of the opening exchange. 'Hallo, dear,' he would call through an open door. 'Are you there?' The bicycle would have played its part in the softening of the meeting. And then it made him familiar in another way. The entire district would know him, no doubt looking on this eccentric anachronism with curiosity or smiling indulgence, even perplexity, or maybe scorn - but certainly noticeable, always unforgettable.

The anachronistic element in Willie was less evident in his earlier ministries, naturally, but it was nevertheless a factor. He did, and continued to do so throughout his life, seem to belong to the nineteenth century. It manifested itself not only in his manner of expression but also in his dress and in his conception of the place and the persona of a minister in the community. In his mind a minister of the church has a position to uphold especially in the figure he cuts. His dress, particularly on Sunday, has importance. He remembers travelling to Castle Donington to fulfil pulpit supply duties as a student in the company of another student who was dressed in morning dress with a 'tall hat'. It had been only in the year that Willie had entered Paton College that the custom for all the students to wear a tall hat was broken. At the time of the journey to Castle Donington Willie was wearing an ordinary sober suit (probably the one made up from Dr. Henderson's gift). He was so impressed with the dignity and elegance of his companion, as he saw it, that when he went to Mexborough he attended church on Sundays in tailed

morning coat and tall hat for morning service and in a frock coat for evening service, but without the tall hat ('the young people would go for a walk after evening service and I did not think a tall hat was appropriate'). At Enderby he continued his custom, although, because the manse was next to the church there was no need to wear a hat. He wore morning dress at morning service, lounge suit for afternoon service and frock coat for the evening. 'But if I had to go visiting in the village after service I would put on my tall hat and if I passed a group of men in the village I would always raise my hat to them.' The village would be well aware that he was about. The rigid stratification of society of pre-First World War had gone forever, but there was enough left of Edwardian paternalism for Willie's conduct and conception of himself as a minister to be unquestioned. However, this dark-suited figure was resonant still of the last century and the people would feel that here was someone who was caught in a vanished era. The paradox was in the contrast between the elements of dress and manner and his attitudes and engaging nature. His Christianity was 'arms spread', his exchanges vernacular and twinkling and, to a degree, self-mocking. You felt that though the manner of dress had been arrived at without self-consciousness, when he had realised what effect he was searching for, then he strove to stress it for all it was worth. He became instantly recognisible and very accessible.

The land around Enderby is fertile. Vegetable and fruit growing was very much the local practice and the new minister was soon persuaded to get his garden into production. The accounts of this vary. Willie says how amazing it is what can be done to keep your vegetable plot in order in half an hour a day. Others say they have no memory of ever seeing him in the garden. Perhaps the half-hours were in the very early morning. Suffice to say there appears to have been a regular supply, especially in wartime when it was in need. And every week someone else would appear 'with something to preserve' from their own gardens.

He was also provided with a clutch of eggs and a broody hen. On one occasion, at short notice, he was asked by Ida to step in as guest speaker to the ladies' fellowship. The appointed speaker had failed to arrive. 'Great Expectations' was Willie's chosen topic. This aroused a great deal of curious interest until well into the discourse when it emerged that the subject was not Dickens' novel, nor the minister's wife, but a broody hen. It seems to have been the cause of some amusement, but I wonder whether the matter was one of regret and even pain for Ida. Not long after they were married she had a hysterectomy. Because of fibroids, her periods were increasingly painful and incapacitating. Willie tackled the issue typically and very quickly. 'This can't be right. I'm sure this is never natural. This is a job for a gynaecologist.' And so Ida's needs were attended to very soon. 'She had suffered in that way since being a child. If she hadn't married me perhaps she'd never have had that done.' Their own attitude to the consequences of the operation, that they would have no children, was that this was God's will, and that this really was a sign that their lives were to be given in service to the ministry.

It was not that God's work precluded a part in the upbringing of children. During the war children were evacuated from the great cities to places less vulnerable to bombing. As a consequence of this, initially three children stayed with the Simpsons for a few days right at the beginning of the war.

They came from the East End of London. This was a temporary arrangement until they were placed along with fifty or more others among the people of Enderby. Willie remembered them as being 'covered with lice'. 'The bed was alive when they left.' A short while later two more children came to live with the Simpsons. They too were from London. They stayed for about six months until the elder of the two boys reached the age of fourteen and 'his father took him back.' The younger one was eight and he was taken back some weeks later. The business of evacuation must have put a considerable strain on children, parents and foster-parents alike. Later there were two others, who stayed for a year. In this instance the fostering was arranged by a minister colleague in Leicester, whose niece in London wanted to place her children in a safe home. Taking on the children also meant that Ida was exempt from war work and that she was therefore free to continue the work of the ministry. The girl, the younger, aged four, had a speech defect. Ida got for herself some perfunctory training in speech therapy so that she could give informed help to the girl. There were three half-hour sessions a day given to practice and training and Willie did his best to ensure that the conversation at the evening meal was turned to those topics which made most use of the sounds presenting most difficulty. 'The cows are in the cornfield round the corner.' There was evident progress. The girl, as an adult, later came to be in charge of a children's home in London.

The boy's educational standard, at the age of nine when he arrived, was well below what Willie thought it ought to be. Never one to miss an opportunity, Willie took advantage of the boy's enforced absence from school for three months because of dermatitis to give him lessons at home in the basics. He helped improve his arithmetic and taught him reading.

How did Willie go about teaching the boy? 'The arithmetic I taught him as I had been taught at school, by rote and repetition. We used to walk about looking at cows in the fields, counting them and adding up the various groups. I used to give him little sessions of ten minutes or quarter of an hour here and there. I don't remember how I taught him reading. I used to write things down for him and get him to read them. I had no blackboard, you know. He was able to read "Pilgrim's Progress" in the end.' I am not sure how much the seventeenth century language invaded his speech but Willie assured me that when the boy returned to school after the three months 'he was of a standard beyond his peers'. I cannot imagine Willie was anything but gentle with his pupil. Certainly there would have been a marked contrast with his own treatment at the hands of Harry Mellor. It would not have occurred to him that his pupil was anything but willing, and he appears to have had an instinctive awareness of the attention span and work capacity of the child.

All these children played their part in the lives of Willie and Ida. It must have been a pleasure for them to have a part to play in the children's lives. Some of the stories to be heard about the plight of evacuees in the homes of people are sad indeed. The motives of some people for taking on the children were at best questionable. The children who found themselves in the Simpson home must have been much happier. It would be stable, loving and warm, the children would know where they stood and there would be more than enough to eat. Not least, these foster-parents knew themselves about hardship and deprivation. On the other hand the children's stays with the Simpsons were relatively brief and though they made their mark, a mark not to be erased, it was as nothing compared to the effect on the lives of Ida and Willie made by Branwen.

Branwen came to the Simpsons when she was twenty days old. The minister in Leicester who had arranged the previous fostering with the Simpsons asked if they would take on this newborn girl for a short while because of the parents' inability at the time to care for her. The baby was her mother's first child. She was only four pounds ten ounces at birth and had to stay in hospital until she was deemed strong enough to come home; she had to reach five pounds. The Simpsons had no hesitation in accepting the child and, when she arrived, everyone rallied round to equip Ida and Willie to meet their new responsibility. The local vicar's wife, Mrs. Hibbert, was especially helpful. All the Simpsons had was 'a dozen napkins'. 'We took out a drawer from the dressing-table, and lined it with a blanket, and put Branwen in it in the middle of the dining table so that she would be safe.' Mrs. Hibbert arrived with a baby bath, a cot and a great fund of useful things which she had accumulated as the mother of three children who had now grown up. More than that, she would 'pop in' regularly to see how things were going. Not that Ida was unable to cope. She was more than competent from the outset, and had a very willing accomplice in Willie. He took his share of all the duties with an affectionate enthusiasm, remembering with dewy-eyed pleasure the joys of cuddling a warm, freshly-bathed and newly-fed babe.

Nevertheless, Mrs. Hibbert's support and interest was very welcome. The Simpson resourcefulness (and economy) ensured that they bought a second-hand pram in the locality, ignoring suggestions in some quarters that they might have bought a new one. 'It's not as if she's our own child.' Branwen's arrival brought a wonderful new light into the Simpson home. Furthermore, the Simpson family back in Chinley took to Branwen with almost equal delight. She became, in Willie's words, 'as their own child'. She stayed until she was nearly five years old. She began school in Walsall at the age of four after Auntie and Uncle had moved to their next ministry, a very lively child who would have none of the practice of the time of being asked to sleep in the afternoons in the classroom. She was bright and intelligent and a source of daily delight for Ida and Willie. She is still his 'little darling'.

One Saturday afternoon, some three months after the move to Walsall, when she was almost five, she went back to live with her natural parents. After her parents had collected her the door to the manse was left open until someone came through it hours later and closed it behind them. Neither Ida nor Willie could bear to close it. Branwen's distress at leaving them was a painful memory for them.'Oh, dear, oh, dear. I shall never forget that day.'

At five to eleven the next morning they received a telephone call to say that Branwen had settled in well. At eleven, morning service began in the church. 'I asked a young man who helped at services to take the service for me and I preached the sermon. I don't know how I did it. I preached extempore on 'Christ Crucified' and then again at evening service on 'Christ's loving kindness'.' The instinct to work off the pain in busy-ness was reminiscent of his mother, Annie, when brother Arthur died. The blow seemed to recall the loss of Arthur.

Branwen was the child the Simpsons could not have themselves. Had they not continued to see her she would still have remained an integral part of their life together. But they did keep contact with her family and were thus able to see her and to watch her progress. They took Branwen and one of her brothers on holiday. They had her and her brothers to stay with them at the manse and spent some holidays with the family. In short, they did everything they could do in order to watch Branwen growing up and to be near to her. But the gap left by Branwen's departure was enormous. 'You know, not a day would pass by without we would mention her. We would say, "I'm sure we should have heard from Branwen by now." or "I've found this ball that belonged to Branwen today." Every Sunday we would come home from evening service and we would sit and talk about her.' The reminiscences must have been bitter sweet.

One day when she was eight Branwen said to Ida, 'Why did you not get another little girl like me?' Ida's answer, which must have cost her dear, was, 'There will never be another little girl like you, Branwen.' For her part Branwen found Ida and Willie to be warm, nurturing (a word she emphasised), affectionate parents. She felt they gave her a good beginning to her life and was grateful to them. She recalled Ida as a person who had given her unconditional care and affection in a very practical way.

It must have taken the Simpsons a long time to recover from the loss. It was worse than a bereavement in that the child was living evidence of the continuing loss. But, counter to that, she was still there and some form of contact was yet possible, contact maintained well into Branwen's adult life when she married and had two daughters of her own. Then she went to live in Scotland and it became so much more difficult for meetings, so that letters and phone calls became more precious. Subsequently Branwen and her family went to live in Australia. Willie was in his nineties when the idea was first mooted and very evidently, it took him some time to adjust. He felt he would not see her again.

Willie believed that we all emerge better for the 'bad patches' in our lives. When were his own bad patches? He thought for a few minutes before he answered and then suggested that his early years when the family was struggling after his father's death were his bad patch. What about the time when they had lost Branwen? He did not reply to this, but in a subsequent conversation, perhaps a year or so later, when the subject came up again, and he was talking with more freedom about it, he remarked how he could not have talked so easily twenty years earlier (nor even a year earlier). It was during that interval of a year that Branwen had emigrated to Australia, and perhaps he felt some sense of release. When he talked about the issue he was earnest, candid about their own and Branwen's feelings at the time and about his own present feelings. But there was no judging of anyone. It is as though the suffering simply had to be.

For the rest of their lives Ida and Willie referred to each other as 'Auntie' and 'Uncle' - their preferred role? Australia is not as far away as it was in Willie's youth. He was able to hear Branwen's voice regularly on the telephone, and the regular correspondence continued. Then Branwen did return, if only temporarily, accompanying her husband, an academic, who had work to do in England. And there was the continuing possibility of further visits, so that in the one sphere where his natural optimism had taken flight, the one sphere where it was most needed, he was still being buoyed up by events he thought to be extremely unlikely, if not impossible.

Jack West was the landlord of the New Inn in Enderby. He and his wife had kept the pub. for forty years, and, according to Willie, 'He had never touched a drop,' apparently following the example of his forbears from whom he had inherited the tenancy. He kept a very orderly house, making a fine judgment as to whether his customers were in a fit state to drink more than 'just another half', and sending on their way anyone who threatened to disturb the equlibrium of the house. The Wests were generous folk. 'You couldn't visit them even for half an hour but that you came away with something - half a dozen eggs, tea or what you will.' The New Inn is a hundred yards or so down the hill from the Congregational Church. Willie would visit the pub regularly and talk with the publican and his clientele, never taking anything stronger than water. He never tasted strong drink in his life. 'I saw too much of the harm it can do.' Willie appreciated the Wests' generosity profoundly. When they would see Ida leaving the village early in the morning to go off to Leicester or even further afield, they knew 'Mr. Simpson will be in at dinner-time'. There would be a dozen eggs waiting. And sure enough he would appear around midday and the conversation would go something like this.

'Hello, Mr. Simpson. Saw Mrs. Simpson going off early this morning.'

'Hello, Jack. Yes she's gone off to Chinley (or Mexborough) for the day.'

'Have you had your dinner, then?'

'Well, no, I haven't yet.'

'Then, perhaps you'd like to sit down with us and have a bite.'

'That's very kind of you. I should love to.'

The entire dialogue was conducted as though for the first time each time and the invitation a pleasant surprise.

Jack West had a good line in picturesque language. Willie's attitude to people who would use bad language in his presence was very relaxed. There are those people for whom swearing is an integral part of their expression, their essential persona. Willie simply acknowledged this and thought none the worse of them for it.

'Jack West used to make good use of the vernacular.'

'Yes, but he were musical,' replied Willie.

The generosity of people like the Wests was especially appreciated because of the war. Some members of the church had relatives in Ireland and were able to supplement their rations with the occasional food parcel. There was an occasion when Ida decided to put on a tea for the missionary society. She was at a loss to see how they could provide, there being only an ounce of butter, quite apart from a dearth of other essentials. The matter was under discussion at a meeting. Willie insisted to Ida that there should be no mention of specifics but when the needs for the tea were broached he lifted an eyebrow in the direction of the Bradshaws. 'And, do you know, a parcel came with all the jolly lot. Providential things happened time and again in Enderby.'

Willie remembered the Enderby pastorate especially for the musical activity of the church. There were regular performances of the Messiah and of Stainer's Crucifixion, for which principal singers were brought in, and there was a high standard of singing at weekly services. The choir would meet once a week to practise and were driven hard by their master, another member of the Young family, a painter and decorator, Ernest. Willie would go in and listen to the practice for the sheer pleasure of hearing the singing and to be educated in the art of the musician. 'Ern' was a character. 'He wouldn't read anything but music and he read that like a book.' He would threaten his choir with throwing his baton at them if they did not measure up to his standards. There were some twenty-five members of the choir, 'all four voices'. They would sing an anthem every Sunday. Willie remembered 'Dudley Buck's "Te Deum Laudamus", which took twelve minutes to render.' The choir led the congregation in chants as well as leading the singing of hymns. With such a substantial choir and a fifty-strong congregation at minimum there must have been a good sound in the church.

Willie thought of the Enderby pastorate as being his 'quietest'. If that were so the others must have been very noisy. There are accounts of all kinds of activity, of tennis, the dramatic revues. They performed 'Cricket on the Hearth', among several other plays and revues. One of the church members, Edna Hunt, was 'a professional who brought the house down in a dialogue called 'Sally's Peppermint' - she was always "Sally" to me after that'. The Ladies' Meeting was chaired by the Minister's wife. 'My wife worked as hard as I did. She was marvellously welcomed all over Leicestershire. She were a marvellous speaker and if she'd put a bag on she'd have looked beautiful.' There was a Men's Fireside which met on Fridays. 'We gathered fortnightly to hear an address on any kind of topic - hospital chaplaincy, art, music - and then we'd have a discussion before the crisp cobs and cheese with coffee. It was packed with men.'

There were also special events, with celebratory and dedicatory services. There was always something to prepare for, a next Sunday, next week, a next event. There would be people who had to be charmed and 'chivvied'. No doubt they would be approached obliquely, their services begged by hint and suggestion. Those who came to know him well would be sure to see the signs before a word was uttered, and would do their service apparently unbidden.

As at Mexborough the Special Events occurred regularly. A particularly notable occasion was held on 28th May 1938. An oak lectern was presented to the church by Jane and Mary Ann Young in memory of their sister Alice who had died on 28th May 1933. Alice Young had been a missionary in what was then Bechuanaland in South Africa at the turn of the century. She had been so highly esteemed by the Chief, Khama, when she married and ceased her work as a missionary that he had made her private tutor to his family. She then became instrumental in helping Khama's wife to become a Christian. In further expression of his esteem for her he had come to visit Enderby in 1895, complete with many members of his family and a large entourage. It is said that the accompanying party was so large so as to ensure that any potential threats to the Chief's regime would be where he could keep an eye on them while he was away from home. The oak lectern was also to commemorate Chief Khama's visit. Willie invited Chief Tshekedi Khama, Chief Khama's

Enderby Congregational Church

THE OPENING OF THE

MEMORIAL VESTRY

the gift of an Anonymous Donor in memory of her Parents, and in gratitude to Almighty God for the Ministry of the Rev. Samuel Haywood, 1856-1862, and the Rev. George Henry Dickinson, 1862-1900

On SATURDAY, APRIL 29th, 1939

at 3 p.m.

son and heir, to come to the service, but, being unable to come, he sent an address to be read out on his behalf.

The extent of the celebration was considerable. The oak lectern itself was designed and made by Jack Bradshaw, a member of the church. Over fifty years later in 1989 Jack remembered making the lectern 'from a piece of oak I found lying around in the timber shed. I jointed the board diagonally and put three metal rods through the top. I was happy to make it for Mr. Simpson.' The programme shows that the celebrations stretched from three on Saturday afternoon, when there was an afternoon service, via a Public Tea at four thirty ('Price 1/-, in the Schoolroom') at which there were 'brief speeches' by six people, four of whom gave anecdotal recollections of Chief Khama's visit. Then came the Memorial Dedication Service, which had three hymns and two anthems, including Dudley Buck's 'Te Deum', a statement on behalf of the church by the church secretary, Mr. J. Shenton, and three addresses. This was Saturday. On Sunday there were two services, as usual for a Sunday, but they were led by a visiting South African minister and the subject of his address was the Khama family. On the Monday the celebration concluded with a 'Valedictory Social Gathering'. There was no point in doing things by halves.

When Willie arrived in Enderby the church had no vestry. He noticed that there was a corner at the back of the church where one could be built. The next question was of raising the funds to pay for it. It soon 'emerged' that there was a benefactress who wished to make a contribution to the church 'in memory of one of her parents and in gratitude to Almighty God for the ministry of Rev. Samuel Haywood, 1856-1862 and the Rev. George Henry Dickinson, 1862-1900' who were the first ministers of the Enderby Congregational Church. This lady made several visits to the church and to the Simpsons, but no-one was ever allowed to know of her connection with the vestry. She would always visit them without pre-arrangement, but Willie always seemed to know when she was due. 'I think we'd better be quick with our dinner today. Lady Anonymous will be here.' Her anonymity has been respected completely. The only person who knew who she was was Willie himself. 'I knew that to reveal her name would spoil the story.' There was naturally a lot of speculation as to who the donor was, and in fact, one man guessed right, but he was given no confirmation. The lady, herself, went to great lengths to protect her anonymity. When the day came to collect the money to pay for the building - the cost was £150 in 1939 - she visited five separate banks so that no-one would be aware where the money came from. The service of dedication was at 3 p.m. on Saturday, 29th April 1939, followed at 4.15 p.m. by a 'Ham Tea in the School, 1/-'. On the following day, for the Thanksgiving Service, the preacher was Rev. Dr. A. R. Henderson, the

Principal of Paton College. His theme was 'Anonymity'. He used the illustration of the monument in Budapest, dedicated to 'all great men and women everywhere.'

On 1st April 1944 a memorial plaque was unveiled in the church to commemorate the lives of Joseph and Eliza Lemmon. 'A man came from abroad and came into the chapel one Sunday night just as we were singing the first hymn, a stranger. By chance he sat in a pew next to an old friend whom he had not seen for many years, when they were in their teens.' The visitor, a member of the Lemmon family, wanted a memorial to his mother and father in the chapel before he went back. So Willie set about arranging a Lemmon Celebration and obtaining the brass plaque that the man wished to be put on the wall. 'I got all the Lemmons to come and we had tea and a service in the schoolroom and goodness knows what. And, you know, it was wartime, a time when lemons were absolutely impossible to get. On the Saturday morning I told the greengrocer that were having a Lemmon Celebration. He said that that was right because he was expecting a consignment of lemons that very day!' The plaque says, 'In loving memory of Joseph Lemmon, who died March 31st, 1918. Also his wife Eliza who died November 25th, 1909. They attended this chapel for many years. Erected by their children April 1st, 1944.'

When the Simpsons arrived in Enderby Willie was in his thirty-seventh year. In the Simpson book all milestones have to be marked. So, three years later, well and truly established in Enderby he celebrated his fortieth birthday, 13th June 1938, by making over a hundred calls in the village. No-one was told that this was his special day. There remains a typewritten list made by Willie of many of the calls he made, with a word or two to describe what he found at each house. Mr. Dimmock in Federation Street ('toes bad') wished him 'good luck'. Mrs. Weston in West Street had a 'smiling face and welcome'. He saw Mrs. Needham of Alexandra Road 'in the cemetery'. Mrs. Cheery was 'not so well, but expressions of appreciation.' Mrs. H. Young of Blaby Road is remarked on as 'a fine singer', with no other comment. There was the lady in Chapel Street who had a 'hard life with husband.' Mrs. Wells of John Street, 'Her sister not well.' But most of the comments speak of the positive response evident among the church members to the Simpson ministry. By the evening the word had gone round that the minister was calling on everyone, and someone made an educated guess to give the reason for his calls. The people were pleased to see him, as much as he was glad to call on them and share his birthday.

'What gave you the idea of celebrating in this way?'

'It came from Samuel Bradbury of Chinley who set out on his fortieth birthday to see how much work he could do. His birthday was in June, and it was a beautiful, bright summer's day. He was a joiner and decorator. He papered two bedrooms.'

To have celebrated his own fortieth in this way gives some insight into Willie's nature. He loved to be in the middle of things, to be the object of attention. One of the chief attractions of the ministry to him was the pulpit which has a strong element of theatre. His sermons, which I shall speak of at greater length later, are self-consciously theatrical and oratorical, though invariably with a homely message whatever the theological thrust of the text. Those who wish to denigrate this facet of him describe it as exhibitionist. Others temper the description with an indulgent smile and say more simply that he is a showman. If the sermons do have a degree of the self-conscious and the contrived about them, in the end the delivered 'package' is the unselfconscious, pure Willie Simpson. Equally there is something unselfconscious, even child-like, about going about Enderby village to hear words of approval on your birthday, and he chose to do that part of his ministry which he enjoyed most of all - the calls on people in their homes. But, with a childlike simplicity he was doing God's work in the manner that God had made him to do it, touching people with his unsophisticated cheerfulness and his optimism, giving pleasure and comfort and receiving it in equal measure. And certainly the people were well used already to seeing his face at the door. Furthermore to do a day's work, following his chosen path, was the same for Willie as Samuel Bradbury's papering two bedrooms.

On the other hand, there is native shrewdness, particularly in the matters of money and of getting people involved in the work of his churches, which were markedly not childlike. When he was interviewed by the Deacons at Enderby with a view to his taking up the pastorate he was asked the question, 'Can you get us out of debt?' The debt was £124 - not inconsiderable in the mid-nineteen-thirties. Joel Shenton, the church secretary said, 'That'll be the man for us!' I wonder if the Deacons were aware then of the extent to which this was their man. When you talk nowadays to the diminishing band of Enderby church members of the Simpson pastorate they remember the activity of the church above all else, and this was a ministry Willie described as 'quiet'. Willie led from the front. He was among the people all the time, starting this, sustaining that, setting targets here, to clear debts and fund new projects, and achieving them there. Their memories are 'that he wouldn't spend twopence if a penny would do'. 'He would go anywhere and ask for money, pubs, anywhere'. 'He was always working, he never tired', and he would always help the people, church members or not.

One man was imprisoned in Stafford Gaol for stealing tyres. Willie visited him regularly during his imprisonment and played a good part in rehabilitation. A couple had to get married 'because the young woman was expecting a child' and Willie stood by them - a theme occurring at other times in his ministry. He visited 'mental hospitals, fever hospitals and sanatoria. And I never left without saying a prayer.' They remembered him 'always about early on his bicycle - cars nowadays stop ministers from being known.' 'He was never without his dog-collar.' There were six cottages in Enderby which belonged to the church. Willie took a full part in painting them and they still never saw him without his dog-collar. He could be very insistent, not to say 'bossy'. The caretaker of the church was given an exact brief as to how he should undertake his duties - 'sweep on Monday, dust on Thursday, when it has settled.' There was a Deacon, deemed by most to be always a 'Johnny Opposite'. They were cleaning around and about the church and the man complained about the cold. Willie offered a silent solution to the man's troubles. As one of the church members said, 'Mr. Simpson, he stuck in well. He just offered him a shovel without a word.'

Others remember the big following of young couples. Willie's predecessor, Rev. S. F. Townley, had established a tennis club. Willie had little sporting ability and no interest in the game of tennis but he saw what an asset the club was to the church. 'Mr. Simpson was not interested in the tennis, just the couples.' 'We had a congregation of both sexes, equally, and the chapel was always full.' 'He knew every age group helped the church. Parents encouraged little children - he encouraged the parents. And once he had you he always kept you. There was always something on. He worked hard and he expected you to work hard. He gave you all jobs to do and got everybody involved.' 'He was so genuine. He took an interest in all the people of the church, all the age groups, especially when he could make a bit of money for the chapel and put it on a sound footing.' They remembered him 'cadging' and cajoling. Mrs. Haynes got herself into the position of being milk-provider for church teas. 'Milk, dear?' Willie would 'ask'. During the war several were kept informed of life in Enderby while they were overseas, across Europe and in North Africa, in a regular flow of letters from the manse. You talk to these people and you hear their unconditional affection and unstinting admiration for the man. The memory is not idealised. They could see the warts, especially in his concern for money. But they knew that the money was watched over for the church and that the 'sound footing' was all.

Ida, too, is remembered with great affection, from the time she sat throughout her new husband's induction service, as was the tradition for the minister's wife, in her black hat with a red rose on it. 'She used to do the sewing, she was such a worker.' 'She was a sweet lady, a lovely person, such a help to him.' 'Didn't she leave a good job to marry him?' She fulfilled a number of offices in the life of the church. Occasionally she would take a service, using to good effect the experience in addressing bodies of people that she had acquired in her life prior to marriage. She was in demand as a speaker around Leicestershire, at church meetings and ladies' gatherings. 'When she were in the pulpit she were as right as ninepence if I were in the back pew,' said Willie. He delighted in the way they complemented each other. 'If she were shinin' I was backin' her. If I were shinin' she were backin' me.' He was convinced that coming into the ministry gave her the opportunity to expand her gifts. But, of course, her most valuable function was the less evident one of sounding board for Willie, and as astute judge of people, whom he found well-nigh infallible, even if its accuracy took some time to be revealed to him. Willie recalled that she felt about Enderby as he felt about Mexborough. It was the first home they had shared. They had worked together to make the manse their own home and to build their ministry among the people of Enderby and she felt at home among them. It held some very sweet memories - and some very poignant ones.

As the years passed by older people in the church would come to Willie to ask about the best way to remember the church in their wills. This, no doubt, occurs in many churches, and was to become a regular feature for Willie in all his ministries. The result in one respect was that he became knowledgeable in the law of probate, even to the extent of doing much of the donkey work on behalf of the solicitor who would then 'rubber stamp' the process when it was presented to him. The solicitor would say, 'How much did you get for this, Mr. Simpson?'

'I got "Thank you very much, Mr. Simpson",' Willie would answer.

Then the solicitor would say to his clerk, 'Write Mr. Simpson a cheque for £5. Think what work he's saved us.'

'I did do it all,' commented Willie. 'All I needed was the Deed of Assent. I used to step up the back stairs at the solicitors and get Dorothy Kind to get it signed.' The word went round the congregation that the minister was only too pleased to offer help and advice in this field. It was a valued service because the people's wishes were treated with respect and sensitivity, and, to the best of my knowledge, their choices were entirely their own. Of course, only passing mention need be made of the 'emergence' of another valuable source of support for the sound footing of the church.

When Willie was at Mexborough there was another earnest young man among the congregation, Roy Booth, whom Willie believed was destined for the ministry. This duly came about and Roy Booth subsequently became pastor of the Congregational Church at Blakenall, in Walsall. It was natural that Rev. Booth should invite his friend and mentor, Rev. Simpson, to come and preach at his church from time to time, and so a connection for the Simpsons with Blakenall was established. Willie had said that he would see his church at Enderby through the war. By now the war was over and though he was not actively looking for a new pastorate - providence was being left to do its work - he must have felt that the natural conclusion to his term in Enderby was approaching. I shall write of the circumstances under which the pastorate at Blakenall became vacant in the next chapter. Suffice to say at this stage that the vacancy did occur, the Deacons at Blakenall made the journey to Enderby to give Willie the call and within two years of the ending of the war he began his third ministry.

Enderby had been another step along the providential path. The contrast with Mexborough could not have been greater in many respects, in the outlook of the people, in the centuries of tradition of the area and in the Congregational Church itself, both community and building. The purpose of his ministry there, nevertheless, was the same. He sought to bring the light of God, made man in the saviour, Jesus Christ, into the lives of the people among whom he worked. God works for man through man. Christ turns no-one away. Repentance and redemption are available all the time. Willie's love of God and Christ are expressed in his love of man, his cheerfulness and his optimism, even in his occasionally blinkered, extremely determined, sense of purpose. This is what the people of Enderby must have seen in him.

They were less needy, less deprived than the people of Mexborough. Historically, in recent history in particular, they had been less susceptible to the vagaries of industry. Life among them had been easier for Willie. But was this entirely due to the different demands posed by the people? When he arrived in Enderby he had had ten years in the ministry. He would have brought none of the residue of the inevitable, initial errors of enthusiasm which had to be carried through the Mexborough ministry. Experience and a clean sheet were useful adjuncts. And, significantly, he had the support of Ida, in her love, her unobtrusive encouragement and benevolent detachment. They were both sorry to leave Enderby, she much more than he. For Willie's part, it had been 'an interval'. 'It had been a happy ministry, but it was too easy. I used to wish for a day like Mexborough.' Going to Blakenall was like going back to his own. He felt there was something to get his teeth into. He felt he could work.

8

BLAKENALL

The incumbent at Blakenall was Rev. Roy Booth. In spite of the church's long history, he was the first minister it had had of its own and it was Roy Booth's own first ministry. He had come to the church as a bachelor to lodge with a family in the district. He was a native of Mexborough and one of the body of people whose young lives had been so touched by Willie's enthusiasm as a new young minister. Willie had seen early that Roy was destined for the ministry, probably before Roy had been aware of it himself. Then Roy had gone to Paton College in Nottingham, like his mentor. He remembered Willie as being 'a breath of light' in Mexborough, thinking so much of him especially for his gift in helping people and for his common touch.

Roy had been given the call by the people of Blakenall after serving a three-month student pastorate towards the end of his college course just as Willie had done in Mexborough. He was one of six children. Willie had given great support to Roy's family. Roy and Willie had great respect for each other and got on very well.

Roy Booth's ministry at Blakenall passed wholly during the years of the

Second World War, having begun in 1941. There was a general acceptance that a minister of the church should not be expected to go and fight in the war, but there were many young men in the Midlands area, as in the whole country, who had been conscripted. One such man in the army was engaged to be married to a young woman, Joy Smith. The Smiths had a long-established connection with the Congregational Church in Blakenall, (still maintained fifty years on). Joy Smith and Roy Booth fell in love and she broke her engagement, ultimately to marry Roy. There were strong feelings in some quarters, not least from her own parents, and this caused a rift in the church. Joy was expected to honour her promise. Others felt Roy was using his privileged position as a non-combatant to take advantage of the absence of Joy's former fiance. He was held to be even more culpable because of his age - ten years or more older than Joy. There was an opposing faction who supported the couple.

When an incumbent minister takes a wife from among his congregation it can place both of the partners in an invidious position. As Willie said, 'She would have remained Joy Smith to many people, as my own wife would have remained Ida Thawley when I married her.' So Rev. and Mrs. Booth decided to seek a new pastorate and found one in Bedminster in Bristol. The Booths were to have a long, happy and fruitful life together in the ministry, serving, after Bristol, in Wiltshire, Staffordshire and Hertfordshire until Roy died in the late nineteen-eighties.

Joy remembered her first meeting with Willie vividly. Sometime in 1943 he came to preach in Blakenall at Roy's invitation. At the time she was not (ostensibly) being courted by Roy. During tea after the service she felt that there was a hidden agenda. Roy had asked her along to be 'looked over' with a view to gaining Rev. Simpson's approval. Approval came, naturally, and the friendship between the two families was cemented, a friendship marked for Joy especially by her regard for Ida. Ida was 'a wonderful support for Willie, a warm, welcoming lady, ordinary, and she had "no side".' Joy admired Ida's intuition and her ability to temper Willie and deflect him by means of good humour from ideas and schemes which were maybe too ambitious. Ida was a good model for the role. Willie said that Joy was to become an equally able minister's wife, providing the support her husband needed and proving her ability to function in the ministry in her own right, just as Ida had done. When she married Roy, Joy was twenty-one years of age. Taking on the commitment of minister's wife is daunting at any age. At the age of twenty-one it must have been doubly so, especially amidst the controversy which the marriage had caused among the folk of Blakenall Congregational Church.

The Deacons at Blakenall had therefore to seek a new minister. Having heard Willie preach already at Blakenall at the invitation of his protege, Roy Booth, and having seen him conduct the Booths' marriage service, the people of the Congregational Church knew something of him. So, in the year when the war was drawing to its end, 1945, he took the Harvest Festival service and soon afterwards they gave him the Call. His first response had been, 'But you haven't got a Manse!' 'We'll build one,' they said. Had the reply come from some quarters, from a church so typically in a chronically parlous financial state, this assertion would have seemed pie in the sky. But it was an assertion made by members of the Smith family.

Congregationalists in Blakenall had worshipped for many years in a small Victorian chapel, now demolished, a couple of hundred yards away from the present church. When it was decided in the early nineteen-thirties to build a new one, the Smiths were the driving force. The stalwart of the church was Fred Smith who, apart from a great faith, had the Midlands self-made man's entrepreneurial drive and self-sufficiency in abundance. He also had five children, most of whom appear to have inherited their father's spirit and determination. William Smith designed the church and Norman oversaw the building work and to an extent the new church was built by voluntary labour.

The project was ambitious. A site was acquired on the corner of Leamore Lane and Chantry Avenue. First they built a school with a large hall with doors along one side opening on to a loggia. The plan was for this hall to serve initially as the place of worship. There were numerous rooms around it, for the various Sunday School classes and the multifarious activities of a thriving church. The footings were also laid for the church itself to be built when time and funds permitted. This has never come about. 'It was a good job it didn't,' was Willie's comment. 'The design was palatial. It would have cost too much money.'

Willie received the Call from the Deacons of Blakenall fifteen months before the day that he took up the pastorate, 1st April, 1947. 'Providence' was at work again. The Mexborough connection with Roy Booth had brought him into contact with the hard-headed drive of the Smiths, people who had energy, saw solutions and not problems, optimists after his own heart. The Manse was not ready for occupation until seven weeks after he took up the pastorate. So they remained living in Enderby and he, Ida and Branwen, who was still with them, travelled over to Blakenall each Saturday to stay 'with the Norman Smith family' until the Monday, Willie having taken the services on Sunday. They moved into a brand new house in the third week of May, 1947.

The Manse is a monument to corporate effort. This, too, was designed by William Smith whose only architectural training had been picked up in his experience as a practical builder. It is a solid, four-square edifice, a three-

bedroomed family house, large enough to allow reasonable entertaining, small enough to be a manageable home. If ever a building reflected the personalities of designer and first occupants this was it. The original proposal was for something ornate, but the new minister was quick to discard this and the only real gesture to embellishment was in the stained glass window on the stairs, designed at the suggestion of Willie himself, illustrating the tools of the various trades which were involved in the building, and the stained glass in the front door which was the fleur-de-lys emblem of the Boy Scout Movement which had an active troop affiliated to the church.

The building of the Manse gave the Simpsons the chance to make their mark in Blakenall before they actually took up the ministry there. Occasions such as the laying of foundation stones, one of which was inscribed to the memory of Fred Smith and laid by his widow, served important purposes. They served to acquaint the congregation with the new pastor and his wife. They gave both minister and congregation an immediate sense of mutual purpose, and in so doing, also focused the minds of the local community on the need for support in the undertaking. Most important of all the minister could lead the people in offering praise and thanks to God for His gifts and opportunities, the essence of everything Willie strove to do.

The building of the house was itself a saga. The time was immediately post war. Building materials were in desperately short supply. The size of houses to be built permitted by law was severely restricted. The authorities were persuaded to allow the 'excessive' dimensions and accommodation of the new

Manse by calling one room, to be the minister's study, 'an educational facility'. Part of the hallway was designated some kind of shrine where cremated ashes waiting to be scattered would be kept. Possibly the ideas were Willie's! After the building was started there were several occasions when a hold-up was imminent, or even actually happened, because the supply of materials had dried up. At one time they wrote to Willie to say they were 'stuck fast' because they couldn't get any lead flashing. His response came, 'It's not tomorrow morning yet. It'll come.' And, of course it did come, 'before tomorrow morning', like a great many of the requirements, because of simple faith (and also because Fred Smith could charm suppliers.)

Willie's first, self-appointed, brief on taking up the pastorate was 'to heal the breach' - a task about which he had no illusions. 'Once people have left a church it is very hard to get them back. They form new loyalties and are loath to break loyalties for a second time. And if you leave out of sympathy and in support of a friend you are very unlikely to return because you have left for no reason of your own.' He acknowledged that over such issues it was difficult to heal the breach completely, but he did start his ministry in Blakenall in the best possible way for him. There was something to do. The new Manse had to be paid for, a responsibility he tackled with characteristic resourcefulness and vigour. Also, for all the satisfaction and the happiness of Enderby, he still felt that among the people of Blakenall he was coming back to his own. The feel was of Mexborough. For one thing, whereas the curtains in Enderby needed washing only once every three months, it was more likely once a week in Blakenall!

When the house was completed the debt was for £1800. It was paid off within a year. The scheme was to regard the entire venture as a ship going on a voyage. The ship was named H.M.S. Forward (is there any other direction?) and there would be a captain, a purser and several of the various ranks. Each deck would be the responsibility of one of the groups in the church and certain groups took on certain concerns. The 'Women's Own' (the ladies' group) undertook to see to the cost of everything 'wet and warm' - the plumbing and the heating. The Men's Fireside Group also, predictably, involved itself in the heating. The Scouts worked to pay for the glass. Others were prevailed upon to make a contribution. The local cinema manager paid for the stained glass window by the stairs. Individuals bought tiles and door-knobs. As Willie said, 'The whole scheme were quite a novelty!' The ship duly came home within the span of a year allotted for its voyage and so there was another Special Occasion, with a service of thanksgiving, and, incidentally, the opportunity to gather in more for church coffers. When Willie first told me of these schemes he was in his early nineties. He surprised himself, in recollecting his own energy and resourcefulness, 'how much I got done in my young days.' He was forty-eight when he moved to Blakenall.

At the beginning of the pastorate the Simpsons went to the same trouble as they had gone to in Enderby to visit as many people belonging to the church as they possibly could. 'The money-raising efforts were not to be allowed to interfere with my ministerial function. And if you don't work, how can you expect other people to work?' The weeks seemed to be even busier than they had been at Mexborough. Enderby had been 'quiet', much of it enforced by the conditions of wartime. Then the years from 1947 were a period of austerity and recovery, but the threat of war had, largely, gone. It was a time of hope for the bright future as well as relief from a gloomy past. People must have been ripe for optimism, seeking opportunity, both of which were readily available from the new minister at Blakenall Congregational Church.

Mexborough in the twenties and thirties had a fairly distant connection with the Sheffield conurbation, being at the end of a string of manufacturing towns and next to the open countryside. Enderby, for all its proximity to Leicester, still kept its village integrity and the open countryside was close at hand. Blakenall, by comparison, as a district of Walsall, was very much part of the urban sprawl of the Midlands, though not far from the periphery.

Next to the Congregational Church site at Blakenall is a school for the under-elevens, of nineteen-thirties vintage. Beyond the school along Blakenall Lane is a small public 'park', a recreation ground. All around is housing. There is no question of a limited availability of people like there is at Chinley Chapel. The housing in Blakenall, Leamore and district is largely from the thirties, forties and fifties, small or medium-sized, semi-detached with garden, often to be found on the outskirts of industrial towns. In such a place was born the garden suburb, the revolt against the claustrophobic, insanitary, terraced streets of the Victorian town. The garden suburb was a conscious attempt to let the sky in, to allow space to breathe and gladden the eye. The optimistic, idealistic impulse which created these new environments became sullied by the demands the Second World War placed on the country's resources. This caused the postponement of the demolition of the terraces and re-housing. When the process could be resumed it had to be done in a hurry and on the cheap with a very evident dilution in the planning and architectural ideals of the thirties. You can see all this around Blakenall. It is hard to see where the real centre is. A community needs a focal point within itself. As you go around Blakenall no striking focal point springs into view.

This factor may or may not have been significant for Blakenall Congregational Church just after the war. The church, as I have said, is an expression of the forward-looking drive of the Smiths and the people whose enthusiasm and industry they tapped. The design is ecclesiastical, without doubt, having gothic echoes for all that it is a single-storey, low building, but it also has the garden-suburb feel of the surrounding housing estate. The site is spacious, the place having been left for the unbuilt church proper, which gave it the sense of a generous use of land which characterises nineteen-thirties housing. In short, it was also an expression, albeit an unconscious one, of the planning ideals of the time, and, having been opened in 1936, there survived enough of this spirit at the end of the war, quite apart from the sheer relief of the ending of the war itself, for the new minister to use to the full. 'A ministry should be a missionary life at home,' he said. 'One should exercise one's life along a truly missionary line and that would yield its own reward.' Under his kind of leadership and example, in such a climate, it now looks as if the way the church community thrived was inevitable. But then it is also easy to imagine what could have happened had there not been a Willie Simpson at the helm.

The terrain around Blakenall undulates but there is not a glimmer of a dramatic climb such as that out of Whitehough. Going about by bicycle would not have been too demanding. So Willie was soon out and about carving a slightly wobbly course through the district with one hand guiding the steed, the other holding the homburg aloft. (His hats wore out at the front of the crown where they were grasped to be raised.) The memories of him are legion. In a wonderful morning of affectionate reminiscence Gwen Smith, Ada Hall, Muriel Law, Joan Harper and Joan Gwinnett, members of the church in Willie's day, recalled a glorious mixture of the precious, the poignant, the uplifting and the hilarious.

'You could go and talk to Mr. Simpson and he would listen to everything you had to say. When you wanted anything sorted out, when you were worried he really would help, and Mrs. Simpson was the same. They had time for everybody.' 'Mrs. Simpson worked so hard sewing and making cakes, and yet you never saw her push herself, ever. She was always in the background, never complained and was always smiling. The manse was always open and always like a palace.' 'He would come to the church for every one of the pantomime performances, sometimes five in a row, and he would laugh before the funny bits came.' 'That little Branwen - what happened? Having her back to her mother broke their hearts. They loved little children.' - in this a deference to the rawness of feeling they must have seen. 'If you're taking the ministry up you've got to be prepared to go out and meet the people and talk to them.' 'Mr. Simpson would go and see people who were bereaved even though they were not from his church.' They remembered how he would use his mother's old nightdresses for laying out the dead. They recalled how he would appear at the back doors of people's houses - 'Hello, dear. Are you in?' He was adept at getting lifts to go on journeys he could not manage by bicycle - 'What shift are you on, Sid? Oh, good. Then you are all right for taking me.' Joan Harper - she was a Keay in the nineteen-forties - told me of the time when the choir came to the back door of their house at Christmas and sang for two hours outside the house while her father played the piano inside. 'It was a cold night, but we collected pounds and pounds from the neighbours. Those were the days when the choir was a choir.' 'And at Harvest Festival Mr. Simpson would go in all the local pubs and collect.'

And then they told me the classic jumble sale story which must have occurred in many church halls. Willie came to help and took his jacket off to act as model for another jacket someone was thinking of buying. When he came to put his own jacket back on it had been sold - for sixpence! He didn't mind their selling it so much as he minded that they got only sixpence for it. Another jumble sale preceded by a month a wedding that was due to take place in the church. The bride's mother and father came to the sale and discreetly enquired of Willie whether there was a dress available which would be appropriate and of the right fit for the big day. He referred them to 'Auntie' (who better?) who used her unerring taste and practicality to find just what was needed. There then came a further enquiry about stockings and shoes which was met equally successfully. Furthermore they found a hat and a handbag, the whole outfit blending, stylish and enhancing to the wearer. Auntie and Ada Hall slipped into the back of the church on the day of the ceremony to see how the bride's mother looked, no doubt pleased with the results of their efforts. What, they wondered, would they read in the local journal about the bride's mother's outfit when the wedding was reported?

They told me about the occasion when Willie ran out of communion wine. It was too late to replace it with the genuine article. What was to be done? The answer was another piece of Simpson ingenuity - a blackcurrant jelly. At Blakenall Congregational Church, as in many free churches, the communion wine is served in tiny 'thumb-nail' glasses. It was a cold morning .... The thought of the communicant vainly trying to empty the glass was irresistible. I asked Ada Hall what on earth she had done under the circumstances. 'Oh,' she said, with a twinkle in her eye and the inimitable resonances of the Black Country, 'Oi just stuck me finger in it and worked it round.'

Willie remembered one wedding in particular, the bride was marrying a man much older than herself, older than her own father, in fact, and there were certain stresses and strains which had to be contended with within the family. People wondered what would be said at the ceremony by the minister. He opened saying, 'This is a unique occasion we shall never forget. It may never happen again. Our three birthdays are on the same day - bride, groom and minister. I'll tell you what. How nice it would be as long as ever we live to write to each other on the day. It changed the whole atmosphere. (And then they had six boys, and I baptised them all.)'

There are many people in the district who remember specific acts of kindness and concern by him. There are stories of loved ones, children in their teenage who were dying from cancer or tuberculosis whom he visited to the end. They would smile 'only for him' and he was the only person for whom they would eat 'because he would sit down and eat with them'. Then he made a garden of remembrance in the grounds of Blakenall Congregational Church for ashes to be scattered. This is recollected with great gratitude but in later years after the Simpsons had left Blakenall it caused problems. The church decided that solely its own members would be permitted to put ashes in the garden. There had been a growing variety of statuary placed to commemorate the departed and no doubt the church felt that there was a limit to the range and number of memorials. When Willie heard of the decision, however, he was very disapproving. To him the turning away of folk from the church, especially at such a sensitive time in their lives, was the beginning of an irreversible, even terminal, decline in the fortunes of the church. He felt that there was a strong argument for compromise: the garden of remembrance should be readily available, but that there should be clear rules about the nature and number of memorials. The resentment was especially strong when the children of a widowed parent wanted the ashes of the other to join the already departed.

Willie's attitude to the remarriage of the divorced is similarly 'free church'. The basis of his view is that if a person wishes to come into church to be married that is sufficient indication of his acknowledgment of God. As Christians we all begin each day with the past behind us. We carry the consequences, even the scars, of the past with us but there is before us each day the choice to be made as to whether or not we let God work through us. Presenting yourself to be married in church, divorced or not, is evidence that you are making the choice, and as Willie said to one man whom the vicar had refused to marry, 'You can't be such a bad chap, or you wouldn't be asking me to marry you. It is sufficient to know that you have found me.' Christ never turns anyone away. Nor will Willie ask any questions about the rights and wrongs of the divorce. 'If a man pours out his soul to you and then he is rejected that is an even worse fate for him. If he wishes to tell me after I have given my consent, then he may do. That is up to him. But it will not alter my consent.'

The fact that his ministry was so much out among the people is illustrated well by the following letter which came in response to a request made through the Walsall local press for recollections of the Simpson ministry:

'Dear Sir,

I were reading the Advertiser news last week. What a surprise I had to see a letter concerning the Rev. Simpson. May I say I knew him when I were a teenager, when he were at Ryecroft Congregational Church. He was a good friend to us in 1951. I had a dear little sister die from cancer at the age of 13 yrs. 11 months He visited my sister often in Hospital, and were a regular visitor to my parents home. Yes he was a familiar man and gentleman with the majority who lived in the area. It brought tears to my eyes when I knew he was still alive at such a grand old age. May I thank you for putting this letter in the news. I found it very interesting. May God Bless him. We all loved him.

Yours Faithfully.'

Ryecroft was a small chapel which was some two miles from Blakenall, near to the centre of Walsall. Like Cannock, Hednesford and Brownhills it received Willie's support. He preached at all these churches on a regular basis and also attended to their pastoral needs. Though he was called to Blakenall to be pastor he took it upon himself, as he did at Mexborough and at Enderby, to give an oversight to congregational churches in the locality which had no minister. They would have no minister for different reasons, perhaps an interregnum, or more likely, that they could not afford a minister of their own. If Willie were preaching there (perhaps once a quarter at evening service or on a weekday), Ida would remain at Blakenall, staying to see that everything went smoothly and 'keep an eye on things'. She would occasionally take a service herself at Blakenall, for example on 'Ladies' Sunday.

Ryecroft was a small, brick-built chapel which, despite its lack of a minister of its own, had a thriving congregation and a strong musical tradition. Nowadays it has become a Seventh Day Adventist Chapel. It is in an area of new and old terraces and of small factories interspersed with derelict land. The retrospective response of the people of Ryecroft especially, and of Brownhills was particularly tender and appreciative of Willie's work. Possibly they were aware that the commitment he had to them was self-imposed. He worked with them simply because he was guided to do so. The area around Ryecroft could well have been reminiscent of Mexborough. Willie recognised the kind of need and knew instinctively how it should be met.

In his nineties there are people from Blakenall, twenty-five years after his departure for Chinley, who are still visiting Willie at his home in Buxworth, some eighty miles from Walsall. They have a long-established tradition of a visit on his birthday in June every year. They bring a meal with them and

arrive in mid-afternoon and there follows a few hours of nostalgia and an account of the current state of their church. After his departure in 1965 the fortunes of the church declined. For whatever reason there was not the steady influx of new blood which any church needs. The people I met spoke wistfully of the loss of his ministry.

In July 1989, soon after his ninety-first birthday, Willie went back to conduct a service at the church for the first time in twenty years. It was a moving occasion. A line of people came in to meet him before the service. There were expressions of uncomplicated joy on their faces as they waited to shake him by the hand and renew a precious friendship. The church was full for his return, uncharacteristically so with its depleted membership, but the word had gone round that he was coming back to preach and so they all came. The child-like pleasure to be seen all around moved us to tears. It was not a revelation to see how he was held in the hearts of his people, but it was an unspoken, irrefutable confirmation of the love and the esteem for him, heard expressed in writing and by word of mouth in a variety of places.

In the days following this visit he was deeply affected. The people of Blakenall, the church itself and the manse were all dear to him each for its own reason. He was eighteen years in Blakenall. This return evoked a mixture of great joy and sadness in him. To see the people he loved in the familiar surroundings he shared with them was an enormous pleasure. On the other hand, to see the church fabric in great need of attention (the roof in the vestry was leaking and there appeared to be neither the will nor the money to tackle the job), to see the grounds and the lawns untended and unkempt and, most of all, to see the garden of the manse fenced off from the church grounds made him very sad. On approaching the church by car, turning into Chantry Avenue, an involuntary 'Oh dear, oh dear' escaped his lips. When he entered the church he wandered round a building which had been part of him for eighteen years, lost for a while, unable to put the numerous small rooms in their context in the building. Then the sharp, critical, Simpson builder's eye began to assess needs and he became fully aware. No doubt, had he been at the helm again another ship would have sailed for a cargo of funds. Soon afterwards he was to meet all the people again. When asked what he remembered of the service the most significant recollection for him was his avoidance of looking at the place where Ida used to sit. For the rest, 'I was in a world of my own.'

The fence around the manse made him very sad. Essentially, the manse, like the minister and his wife, must be accessible. To cut them off, put a barrier around them, is a repudiation of what they were there for. His spontaneous, instinctive anger at the sight of the fence, expressed with a momentary fierceness and a contrasting compassion, spoke eloquently and concisely of his attitude.

A day in Blakenall, as ever, started for Willie early in the study. The sermon had to be got ready, the priority for the morning. In the afternoon there would be the five visits to be made, 'and if you didn't manage five visits on one day you made up for it on the next day.' There were, of course, weddings, funerals and baptisms to conduct and to prepare for, and then, during his fifth year in Blakenall he became chaplain at Manor Hospital in Walsall. Every evening of the week had its obligations. There were Deacons' Meetings, choir practices, the round of social gatherings which any thriving church generates - whist drives, old time dancing, and so cn. There were Girl Guides and Brownies, Boy Scouts and Cubs, as well as the theatrical productions which became a hallmark of the church. There was an annual gala day, an affair which he instituted, with a queen chosen by the children themselves every year. 'I could always tell which girl they would choose,' said Willie. Although he was not directly involved in many of these activities he felt it to be his duty to show an interest and it was certainly much more than a token interest. Many of the functions did make money for the church and we know very well how important he felt it to be that the church should be solvent, but the prime purpose, even in matters which were straightforwardly to raise cash, was to involve people in a joint purpose, to bring them together - in short, to promote fellowship. In this respect he knew that fellowship reached out beyond the

The crowning of the Rose queen at Blakenall.

bounds of his congregation. He would go into the local pubs at Harvest Festival time not simply to ask for the patrons' financial contributions but to be there among them. 'Have a pint on me, pastor,' they would say. 'That's very kind,' he would reply, 'but, no thank you. I only touch water, and that not too strong.'

The duties of being chaplain meant that he visited the hospital on two mornings a week. He made sure that he spread his ministry into every conceivable corner of the hospital community. It was not only the patients to whom he gave attention. The entire staff, nurses, hospital secretary, porters, laundry workers, doctors were greeted and blessed. He never forgot the laundry workers - 'Now there was a dirty job'- and made a point of visiting them every week. One nurse, a sister on a maternity ward, Ivy Heslop, recalled 'his energy, his commitment and his warmth. Patients would wait for his cheerful and comforting words irrespective of belief or denomination.'

On his first visit to the hospital he went into the canteen at lunch-time for a meal and made the acquaintance of an electrician, Norman Richards. This developed into a firm friendship which was sustained in his old age. They ate lunch together twice a week during the entire length of Willie's chaplaincy. Norman treasured this friendship and had memories of interesting conversations over the lunch table and of the services which Willie would conduct over the hospital broadcasting system, fifteen to twenty-minutes. 'I would play a short voluntary at the beginning and at the end of the broadcast on the organ they had there, and I would give a little address and offer prayers,' said Willie. Norman presided over the technical side. Willie was very conscious of the fact that he was diverting the electrician from his vital duties, and also of the fact that, as a non-conformist he might have been seen to be imposing his own brand of Christianity at the expense of others to a captive audience. As a result he decided to discontinue the broadcasts after only a short period, though not without hearing the gratitude for the inspiration he had been to one patient, a man who said that the first voice he heard as he regained consciousness after an operation following a traffic accident was Willie's. He felt it had set him on the road to recovery.

Ida and Willie visited the Manor Hospital every Christmas Day during the eleven years of his chaplaincy there. They stayed until they had eaten their Christmas dinner. They went home 'in time for the Queen's speech'. They had their own Christmas meal on Boxing Day. On the first occasion he visited on Christmas Day they went to one of the ward sisters and asked if there were anyone especially poorly. 'All those who stay in on Christmas Day are poorly,' she said. On one occasion he found a couple sitting by the bedside of a sixteen-year-old boy who was very ill with a cancer of the eye. Willie promised the parents that he would return to see the boy when he had finished making the rounds. When he did so some hours later the parents had gone home and subsequently the boy had died. The ward sister asked him if he would take the news to the boy's home, a task which remains sharp in his memory. The parents were prepared for the news, but to be asked to carry it to them on Christmas Day was heavy.

While doing his chaplaincy work there was an incident which recollected something of the ancient animosities between the established and non-conformist churches. Willie visited all the wards in the hospital, including the maternity ward. Here he shed his light and shared the pleasure of mothers and fathers. On the other hand he did not shirk facing the inevitable grief and dismay after a miscarriage or a still birth. He offered prayers for 'courage and strength' to meet what lay ahead.

One mother, not a churchgoer, was visited after she had gone home by her own minister, a Church of England vicar, who broached the question of 'churching'. She told him that she had already said prayers with Mr. Simpson, innocent of the implications of his prayers in the context of churching. For Willie's part, he had offered the prayer as he would have offered it for anyone in hospital, at home, in the street, in their cars, anywhere - to give thanks for

God's grace and to ask for God's blessing. The vicar took it that this was a free church minister who was out to usurp his function in the life of one of his parishioners and brought the matter up indignantly with members of the Free Church Council, suggesting that the matter should be reported to the hospital committee. He was advised against any further action. They knew that the committee thought so highly of Willie that the vicar would do nothing but reduce his own standing with them. Probably they also tried to enlighten him about the spirit in which the prayers had been offered.

It is rare to hear Willie speak ill of anyone. He usually shakes his head expressing a mixture of perplexity and resignation at anyone's aberrations, but he will say nothing. The spirit of tolerance and of Christian forgiveness is large in him. On the other hand he saves outright disapproval for ministers who fall short of his own standards of conduct and principle. It could be said that the Anglicans start at something of a disadvantage with him. This probably had something to do with 1662, and with their failure, in his view and in some cases, to be fair about the fees due for committals he has presided over in Anglican churchyards. On the other hand, those vicars who are fair (and hand over the fees due) and conduct themselves in a truly fraternal way, notably Rev. Victor Hibbert at Enderby, could not have enjoyed greater regard from him. He never can understand why ministers of any persuasion keep themselves apart from the people. Visiting people in their homes, being out and about amongst the flock, as this story stresses, is, for him, integral to the ministry of a man of God, and the aspect of Willie's ministry always mentioned when you talk to his people. The solely contemplative life of some orders of monk and nun are beyond his comprehension.

I do not know whether Willie ever thought explicitly about the way he would be a minister and carry out his round of duties. Very likely he simply followed his instincts and used the naturally gregarious nature, the strength and the tenacity that God gave him. He could not have done the job in any other way. The joy and the satisfaction in heeding the call came from the opportunity to live out his faith in direct daily contact with the people. The less tangible aspects of faith, the spiritual relationship with God, the intellectual challenge of theology, the leadership of the congregation in prayer and praise are all very important for him, but certainly of no more importance than the expression of God in Man by his daily deeds. Nevertheless there is a paradox in the contrasting expectations he has for lay people on the one hand and for fellow ministers on the other. He placed great demands on himself in terms of effort and principle. He has high expectations of his colleagues. His compassion for them is easily eroded if they fall short. For the world at large the chance of repentance and redemption is always there. For the minister who errs in his view he finds it harder to be forgiving.

'Erring' could mean simply not being available to the flock on a Simpson scale, or of not showing the energy and commitment to maintain 'a sound footing.' The analogy is with the severity of the law in dealing with the fallen policeman. However, the strength of his belief is such that, in the end, there is no denying the needs of any human being whatever the steepness of the descent from grace. Compassion for the unsatisfactory minister would have been slower in coming. It is hard for Willie to accept that none of us, especially a minister of the church, is all things to all men. That same variety of talents which he was so adept at harnessing in his church communities exists equally in the ministry. We cannot all be sociable and extravert. There is a need for the rigour of the ascetic. There is a place for the contemplative. We all have a part to play.

Nevertheless Willie would assert that he would have 'the greatest sympathy' for anyone who had fallen from grace. He spoke of Peter in chains and 'listening for the music in the clanking of the chains'. He recalled once giving a sermon on the very theme and a visit immediately afterwards by a young man whose girl-friend was expecting a child. He told Willie that he was 'in chains', that he would have to get married, with no money, no home and no prospects. Willie's immediate instinct was to 'stand by them', 'keep them on their feet', and all this in the face of disapprobation from other members of the church congregation. To the person who gave voice to the disapprobation he asked the simple question, 'What would Christ do in these circumstances?' - a question he had to ask three times before the point was conceded. 'What's more,' said Willie, 'these two people became life-long stalwarts of the church.'

The place of providence, or fate, or even coincidence in our lives is a matter for long conjecture. How is it that we are in a particular place at a particular time to encounter a particular person? How is it that this person may fill a need in us, maybe in providing a necessary testing of our mettle or even bringing solace from an unsuspected quarter? Why do we set off on the journey of each day, despite some sense of security in our expectation of its destination, unknowing of the diversions and calls that will interrupt it? Why is it that the testing that some people or events submit us to is beyond our bearing? And yet we can look on others who are asked to endure what appears to us to be so much more and see them not simply surviving but emerging all the better for it.

The answer to such questions lies, of course, less in the severity of the problems that the people and the events present, more in the capacity of the individual to deal with them. For a man like Willie Simpson providence meant opportunity. A person should be able to remain open to experience, to allow things to happen, to follow instinct, to go with the grain of happening. And when opportunity bids it needs to be recognised and used.

There are those blessed individuals who see opportunity at the very point when to others all avenues have been sealed, and the phrase 'to have no option but to..', instead of indicating a narrowing of choice, becomes the precursor to the most positive of action. Willie talks of providence at every stage in his life, even at the darkest of times such as when Branwen was taken back to her natural parents, when life must have felt very bleak for him and for Ida. I know that the way they must have dealt with the enormous blow would have been to have thrown themselves even more wholeheartedly into their pastoral work, to have numbed the pain by being busy and occupied. They also came to try to protect each other from painful reminders by removing from newspapers any accounts of missing or abducted children, neither aware for a long time that the other was doing the same. But his reaction in the late years of his life in recalling the time, showed that when the door of the manse closed behind them and they were alone together they grieved the loss of their little darling in a very real sense. 'Every Sunday night when we came home from the service we had our supper and we talked an hour about her.' They must have acknowledged each other's grief, which is a good thing, because the continuing growth in their ministry thereafter would not have taken place had they not done so. The events of this time are etched in Willie's memory in his old age, but, though he speaks of the trauma in graphic terms, it is a time from which he recovered and he will assert that it was a providential 'bad patch'. I can only speculate on the significance of the loss for Ida. Was she as apparently resilient as Willie? If the accounts of her bearing, her dealings with all the folk in Blakenall and Chinley, her ministry, are anything to go by, certainly she did not wither from then on.

Willie said that 'the experience of Branwen made us much more understanding.' And though it was at the time 'worse than a death' he said that in later years as they were able to watch Branwen grow up, hear of her developing education, watch her life unfold and see her have a family of her own, the loss became bearable. In his old age he would say, 'It's forty-one years (or however many) since she left and there's never a letter or card that she's sent but what's preserved.'

During the course of this narrative Willie's mother has appeared only in the context of her influence and her guiding hand in his formative years. In fact, she remained as a figure of great importance to him throughout her life and she lived until she was nearly ninety. Not long after his leaving Paton College he was able to buy for her the house in Portland Grove in Chinley, a testament not only to his concern for her welfare and security but to his own ability to accumulate enough money. On the other hand, though, a man who can put together his first shilling of savings from meagre wages should not be underestimated. As a student and as a young minister Willie's mother was the lodestar of his life, the sounding board and the support, at least until he married Ida.

When Ida became the minister's wife there was apparently no traumatic usurping of Annie, more an assumption of complementary functions. Mother changed hers to meet the new situation. She had given her approval of her son's choice of a wife almost instantaneously when Ida was introduced to her, and knew full well that her own enabling instincts would be better served if she encouraged the partnership to flourish. Both Ida and Annie were

Willie with Ida and his mother.

personalities in their own right. Probably, the circumstances of Annie's life, especially when left to bring up a young family alone, would have prompted a more overt assertiveness in her, but Ida had her own strengths and an ability to exercise them subtly. According to Willie they got on very well together. Willie and Ida visited his mother regularly and always spent at least part of the Christmas holiday with her. There are records in church minutes of the minister's notice that he would be away for certain Sundays in order that he should be going home to Chinley. Willie found Ida's people equally accepting and warm.

Willie and Ida had lived in Blakenall for about a year when they decided that his mother should come and live with them. She was with them for four years until her death in 1952. During that time, possibly a year or so after her arrival, Ida's mother came 'for a short stay' and remained with them for eighteen months until her death.

It must be a harmonious household that can accommodate two mothers-in-law. The two of them seem to have enjoyed each other's company very much. They shared the same birthday, 21st June, and were similar in age. Their natures were complementary. Ida's mother was very talkative and had a great fund of stories, most of which Ida had heard before (and was not well disposed to hear again). Willie's mother had the capacity to listen and a store of prompting phrases which expressed interest and helped the narrative along. Willie believed that she actively enjoyed the stories and would laugh out loud at them. 'They were real friends,' said Willie. The presence of both in the house made it possible for Ida and Willie to feel that they could safely leave them to attend to their duties beyond the home.

Ida's mother died after eighteen months with them, a short illness taking her quickly. Willie's mother lived for another two or three years. She died peacefully at one o'clock on a Sunday morning after a steady but unprotracted decline. She died of 'old age' and had been ill for about six weeks. Willie took one of the nightdresses that Annie had kept to serve as a shroud and together he and Ida laid his mother out. At two-thirty they then went back to bed. The arrangements for her funeral at Chinley Chapel were made before the service on the next morning. Willie made no mention of his mother's death at either morning service or at Sunday School in the afternoon. In the evening he altered the order of service, preaching the sermon soon after the beginning instead of towards the end. During the sermon he said that 'Mother had taken her flight at one o'clock this morning.' His text for the sermon was 'He that plougheth, plougheth in hope' - given in the context of 'Sunday School teachers, stalwart members of the church and mothers.' Why did he leave the announcement until the evening? 'It was the right time. We avoided sympathy during the day. We could go home after the service with no other duties. We went home and we were together.'

Earlier in the year (this was September) Willie had been invited to conduct the Harvest Festival service at Chinley Chapel. He had expressed his concern to his mother that they would not be able to leave her. 'Take the service,' she said. 'We'll all be there.' Annie Simpson was buried in the family grave in Chinley Chapel churchyard with her husband, Zachary, her son, Arthur and generations of Simpsons, nearly fifty years after becoming a widow. Willie took the service of committal. Willie's brother, Frank Pearson, her son by her first husband, dug the grave.

Willie's account of his mother's funeral is vivid. For him it was by no means a sombre occasion. For him no funeral is sombre. 'A funeral is not a sad occasion. You approach with a determination to brace, to build up, to buck people up - give something to uplift them.' He remembered the funeral of a gardener of whom he said, 'Our friend is not dead, but transplanted to soil tended by the divine gardener.' His attitude to his own mother's funeral was similar. He was deeply thankful for a long life well lived, and because their relationship had been essentially loving and giving there was no unfinished business between them. Significantly, the service of committal and remembrance was in his 'beloved sanctuary', Chinley Chapel. 'As soon as we opened the church door and I preceded the coffin saying the words, "I am the resurrection and the life, says the Lord. He that believeth in me shall never die..," I was uplifted. It was a wonderful occasion. There was no grief. The presence of God lit the place up. There was such a sense of thanksgiving. I conducted the service as a fulfilment. There was not a sorrow in my heart. How happy I was that Mother had arrived home. And it was the chapel that took the sorrow away.'

Some four years after Branwen's leaving, and not long after the interval during which the two mothers had come to live with them, a young man came to take up his first teaching post in Palfrey, a town centre district of Walsall. Trevor Rush was a music teacher, a practising Christian. His family originated from Conisborough, only a few miles from Mexborough. We know what a special place the people of that district had in Willie's heart. Trevor found that Blakenall Congregational Church was looking for an organist in the 'Situations Vacant' column of the local press. There was an immediate rapport between him and the minister and his wife. For six months Trevor played at Blakenall at both morning and evening service. Then he played at Blakenall in the morning and at Ryecroft in the evening. He spent all or part of the afternoon at the manse. One evening Willie called on Trevor at his 'digs' and was surprised to find that he was confined to an attic room without heating,

Trevor Rush at Ryecroft with the choir

except for meals. A day or two later Trevor told Willie and Ida that he was looking for alternative 'digs'. 'Did they know of any?' Willie has a clear picture of the unspoken communication between himself and Ida. Trevor was offered a bedroom and became 'the son of the manse'. In Trevor's words, 'Willie seemed to feel that God had sent me to fill the void left by Branwen's sudden departure.' He stayed with the Simpsons for six months until he was able to take up another teaching appointment in Devon near to his family home. His departure brought back the same kind of emotions they had felt when Branwen had gone. The friendship continued and they were able to spend holidays with Trevor's family in Torquay.

The six months in the Simpson home gave Trevor Rush a special insight into the way the home worked. It was a real home from home, a welcome fireside, meals 'like mother used to make', conversation, company and humour. He draws a picture of Willie which contrasts markedly with that of some parsons whom Trevor describes as 'invisible during the week and incomprehensible on Sundays.' He remembers breakfasting on bacon and egg every day, the black homburg and the dark clerical garb, and the trusty steed, Willie's dependable old roadster which would take him along and down a visiting list 'as long as your arm', no responsibility ever shirked. Willie was, in Trevor's words, 'a colourful character and an anachronism but people loved him for it.' Above all Trevor remembers the love and the kindness, the warmth of the Simpson home.

Willie recalls that Trevor hardly went out in the evening in the six months he was with them. He prepared his school work, kept them company and played the manse piano for them. A particularly favourite piece for Willie was the Gigue by Corelli, which he remembered Trevor playing 'perfectly' and then 'with his soul in it' - and 'What a difference! He also played us through all the great oratorios, Handel's, Bach's, Haydn's, Mozart's.' Trevor filled one of their needs but their need was also his. They were brought together for a purpose and because Willie and Ida knew instinctively that to go with God's grain would serve the purpose well.

The question of Willie's awareness, or not, of the figure that he cut, the impression he made, has been considered before. The answer developed as he grew in his ministry and as he got older, a complex issue which needs answering again in the context of this succeeding ministry in Blakenall. Basically Willie sees a sole purpose in his life - to minister to the people, to express his belief, his faith, through the way he lives his life. This he did with a paradoxical lack of self-consciousness on the one hand, and an acute awareness of his role in society as a minister of the church, on the other. This had had a significant part to play in his choice of a wife. She had to be a minister's wife as well as the woman he chose to spend his life with. Inasmuch as he was alive to his role as a minister and the status it carried, as has been said, the figure cycling around Mexborough, Enderby, Blakenall and Chinley was consciously cultivated and an expression of the showman in him. The role of minister as he saw it also dictated a flattening of his vowels (when he saw fit) and a vocabulary and sentence structure redolent of the nineteenth century pulpit. School children were 'scholars'; pound notes remained 'sovereigns'. But there was no resisting the Willie Simpson from Chinley for very long. The Derbyshire vowels, the dialect, the informality, directness and kind humour would break through and because he identified more easily with the folk of Blakenall he could reveal the Derbyshire Willie more readily.

Trevor Rush remarks on the 'contrast between the sombreness of his attire and the colourfulness of his personality'. The dog-collar does place the parson apart in the community. That is undeniable. But whereas there are ministers who seek to minimise the impact of the collar, Willie, at the other extreme, used his dress, and not merely on Sundays, almost to give a bravura performance, to use it and go through and beyond the natural eccentricity and capitalise on it for the good of his fundamental cause. The bicycle was an essential part of the picture.

There was another, very practical reason for his preference for the bicycle. He was hopelessly unmechanical and impractical. Only once did he try to mend a puncture on his bicycle. His experience was such a bad one, taking him hours of fruitless effort, that he gave up the idea of ever trying again, which was completely out of character. The nearest bike shop or competent friend was left to do the job.

By contrast, Ida had the practicality and practical common sense. 'She mended the fuses.' For Willie the lack of practicality meant that anything that demanded a more complex skill such as riding a motor-bike or driving a car was utterly beyond him. The possibility of owning a car hardly occupied a moment's thought. For one thing the economics of car ownership were insuperable. A car would be a wholly unwarranted expense. It was not unknown for him to put his bicycle on the back of a lorry and join the driver in his cab for some longer journeys. He did once, while at Blakenall, acquire a 'mo-ped', for £27. It lay in the outhouse behind the manse for a few weeks until the caretaker of the church persuaded him that it would be better to learn how to ride it. There followed a series of lessons in the grounds of the church which served only to highlight his ineptitude. Little progress was made. The last lesson finished with the front wheel of the machine wedged between the railings by the Garden of Rest. There was a trail of tyre straight across the Garden of Rest. Not long afterwards a student from Handsworth College came to preach and asked in the vestry after the service whether they knew where he could find a cheap motor-bike. Norman Smith, without consulting Willie, told him it would be better if he took the one the church had 'before our minister gets killed.'

Like the message he had to take on Christmas Day as a hospital chaplain many of his visits to people were in times of trouble and need. What were Willie's feelings about such visits? He spoke of pride on the one hand and humility on the other. The pride, a surprising feeling for a Christian at such times, he explained as 'stemming from his association with the people, from the opportunity to be in the presence of God with them at their time of need, and from having a calling which put him in a place where he could be of use.

The humility - 'the apron of humility' that Paul speaks of - arose from 'standing in the face of good folk who sustain their own wholeness with God's help when they are at their lowest.' The image of the apron appeals very much to Willie. 'A workman wears an apron as he bends before his work. Even a bishop wears one.'

He must have visited homes in travail on countless occasions. No doubt his manner in the face of such situations was honed and refined over the many years of his ministry and it can only be surmised how he would have conducted himself as an inexperienced young student. Possibly there would have been some awkwardness. He had been about his pastoral work from an early age and in deportment and manner had been regarded as far beyond his years well before he even became a student. The obvious evidence is the response of the people who had the benefit of his ministrations in the four places of his ministry. Many speak of the special appropriateness of his prayers, offered generally as he left. Others recall the unaffected openness and directness in the face of issues and fears. The over-riding memory is of sensitivity, warmth and kind concern. In later years some people felt that he would 'go into automatic pilot' and that he would take recourse to stock phrases which perhaps made them feel that he was not really alive to their problems. For them Ida was a better resource. 'Now, she really understood,' they would say. However, throughout his long life Willie enjoyed his ministry - in all its aspects. To give help gave him great satisfaction. When we do good there is invariably something in it for ourselves both at the time and in the reputation that it can generate and it would be deluding to say otherwise. That is not to devalue the good that is done. We all have a choice. We can look at what we can give or we can be preoccupied with what we can take. Willie found satisfaction and the heartfelt appreciation of his people in what he gave.

Hanging on the the chimney breast of the sitting room of his home in New Road, Buxworth is the cross and chain which was used to consecrate the life of Ida in the service of the ministry when she and Willie became engaged in Mexborough. He wonders who should inherit this cross. There were three people who had an intimate part to play in Ida's and Willie's life together. They all had the special place in the heart reserved for the young. There was Branwen, of course, and Trevor. There was also John Biddulph. John another musician, and teacher, who became organist in the late nineteen-fifties at Ryecroft Church before he was twenty years of age. He came to visit the manse regularly, in the course of his duties as organist, but was increasingly attracted by the warm welcome and the affinity that he felt to Ida and Willie. He came to spend many Saturday evenings at the manse and remembered sitting there, just the three of them round the fire, scarcely a word spoken for long periods, but with a palpable rapport in the room. As the time approached eleven o'clock and Willie was beginning to express concern that John should be going home there would be a little game. John had already accepted a tacit invitation from Ida to stay till Sunday morning and the mere fact that he was making no moves to leave revealed to Willie that he would be staying. There would be cry of pleasure from Willie - yet again a surprise! John became the third 'child they could not have' and they became to him Auntie Ida and Uncle Willie. 'We practically adopted him!' To this day he is 'Uncle Willie' for John Biddulph.

Nowadays John Biddulph thinks of the Willie of nearly thirty years ago as 'a big man', not that he was especially large in stature. John particularly recalls his presence in the pulpit. He knew him to be an orator and like Trevor Rush and others who have been within earshot of the Simpson house he knew that sermons were meticulously prepared, not simply in content but in delivery, which was rehearsed in terms of volume, pace, pronunciation, nuances of tone and even the different voices of protagonists in the representation of scenes of conflict. There were times when they wondered how many people there were in Willie's study even when their eyes had told them that only he had gone into the room.

John liked Ida. The rapport between them I have already spoken of. He remembers her warmth, her kindness and concern, and her impeccable taste in dress, such a source of wonder and admiration for Willie. John remembers her 'wonderful' hats especially. He accompanied the Simpsons on several holidays, the most memorable being a tour of Scotland when they were in their sixties. The basic plan was to go 'up the right hand side and down the left-hand side of Scotland', a plan accomplished in a week or so. On the way up they decided to stay in Windermere in the Lake District for a night, but found that there was no accommodation to be had. It was the height of the summer and they had to sleep in the car. Willie was reminded that he had put a couple of pillows in the car as an afterthought as they were about to set off and he marvelled at his own presentiment. The other marvel is the picture of the party asleep in a car - an elegant elderly lady, a parson resplendent in his dark clerical garb and their young chauffeur.

Willie has always carried notions of a wayfarers' code. This meant that as a traveller you are entitled to expect a degree of courtesy and help from folk you prevail upon. Such help is not requested wantonly nor impolitely - on the contrary the requests will be couched in the linguistic conventions of the nineteenth century, or earlier. He will not ask too much. The limit of his needs will probably be hot water for the tea he carries. By the end of the Second World War, perhaps into the fifties, only travellers such as tramps would knock on doors and ask in this way. In the sixties people would not really expect to be asked for this kind of help. 'Respectable' people brought their tea in a thermos flask, or stopped at the roadside cafe. Spending money in cafes, on the other hand, is not done lightly by Willie Simpson. And so it was that Ida, Willie and John Biddulph, called at a house in Selkirk for hot water. There was a man in the garden. The clerical garb must have played its part. Very soon the encounter developed into a full-scale invitation to share a meal. There was a piano in the house and John, the musician, an ardent Gilbert and Sullivan enthusiast with a good tenor voice, director of a local operatic society, was asked to play. Their hostess was herself a G. & S. aficionado. They sang the repertoire together in an impromptu concert which left them all glowing. The wayfarers' code has many rewards.

The holiday continued on its planned course. John O'Groats was a disappointment. 'I expected heaven to come down when I got there,' said Willie, 'but it was a very ordinary place.' One of his characteristics, particularly evident on holidays, was his wish to go to the top of, get to the end of, find the source of, mountains, peninsulas, rivers, or to find the special place in a church or a gallery of which he had read (often in Talmage's sermons) and which 'was a sermon in itself.' So, if you go to Scotland you go to the end of Scotland and getting to the end could be expected to have some mystical significance - not always fulfilled.

When they had done their tour and were back in the Lowlands, Willie recalled that there were still gaps in his 'collection' of English cathedrals, having visited almost every cathedral in England. Salisbury was missing from the collection. He asked John if it would be possible to complete the collection 'on the way home'. Home was in Walsall in the Midlands, about half way between the Scottish border and Salisbury in Wiltshire. John's love for 'Auntie and Uncle' made it impossible to refuse the request. They duly visited the cathedral, which, incidentally has the tallest spire in England (but you cannot get to the top of it), and while in Salisbury Willie took the opportunity to visit his brother, John.

The Blakenall ministry was in many ways a period of awakening. It had begun in the immediate post-war period at a time of austerity, restriction and then nascent recovery. Gradually society was restoring itself materially and there was a consequent growth in opportunity. The demands of the district were such that made Willie feel he had a 'real job' to do. And because he had arrived there at a time of growth, as a symbol himself of the will to develop the church community, it was ideal ground for him to grow his schemes and his projects. He had instituted the annual gala ('which financially kept the cart on the wheels') and the church buildings were humming with activity every night of the week. The Sunday School had so many children that one teacher suggested that they should post a notice stating that it was not able to take any more. Willie would have none of this - no-one is ever turned away. 'We shall pack them in somewhere. And, do you know, we never did get much bigger. We were always able to cope comfortably.'

A development after his own heart was suggested to him by Frank Smith (another Blakenall Smith), a Scout Master and a college teacher in engineering, a practical man. There were ex-R.A.F. wooden barrack buildings for sale. They could buy one for £30, and with the great fund of skill and building expertise among the church members, erect it, provide it with all the necessary services, and thereby add a useful resource for the social life of the church. Willie listened carefully to the proposal, thought a while, and then said, 'Proceed, Frank! We'll pay for it in three years!'

This was another project invaluable as much in the travelling as in the arrival. Here was another opportunity to harness energies, to motivate, to lead and to get money to follow. So, he left the building to those who could build and took upon himself the task of making sure the project was paid for in the three years he had aimed for. It was paid for in no more than one year. When it was ready it was opened ceremonially by Mr. Rubery Owen, a prominent Midlands industrialist, who, during the celebratory meal asked the treasurer if it was all paid for. The treasurer replied that they were well in hand. Willie thought this to be a good example of looking a gift horse in the mouth and believed a golden opportunity had been lost. However, he mentioned later to his distinguished guest that the kitchen needed fitting out and 'a sizeable donation came.' The New Extension became an important and well used resource for the church. It stood, over thirty years later, in good condition, a monument to the conscientious skills of the volunteers. The parquet floor which they put down was something to behold.

The minutes of Deacons' meetings at Blakenall, like similar minutes from a thousand churches, reveal that the bread and butter of the business of the meetings is far from spiritual. Much of the matter under discussion concerns the fabric of the church and, of course, how the need to keep it can be met financially. Needless to say, such matter was meat and drink to Willie, but it did not divert him from a regular and pointed concern with the spiritual and the pastoral when the need arose. At one meeting in the early fifties he was evidently earnestly seeking ways of making the Deacons' participation in services more significant. (Deacons in the free churches are lay people who are elected from the church membership, charged with such responsibilities as maintaining a place of worship, of overseeing the church's finances, of giving leadership to the congregation, particularly in their example of service, and of representing the church in the wider community. They are lay officers dealing largely with the church's secular affairs.)

There is a minute (in the Minister's own handwriting) which records the Minister's speaking of 'the vital necessity for Deacons to meet in the vestry both before and after services. If the right atmosphere was to be given to a service the vestry was the place to apply the power. What greater inspiration to a minister than to find the vestry filled with Deacons waiting to welcome him and to offer a short prayer before he leaves to start the service? Nothing is more necessary than "May God bless our service." What an effectual prayer such can be!' This exhortation appears to have been the culmination of a campaign which had been started by the Minister's suggestion that Deacons leave their hats and coats in the vestry before the service. 'They could then be brought together at the end for a 'good-night' to the Minister.'

In the early fifties Willie proposed to the Deacons what was called a 'Forward Movement'. Its priorities were to be '1. Loyalty. 2. Welcoming strangers to church. 3. Visiting the sick. 4. Seeing what was wrong and putting it right, not just talking about it.' If ever four concerns expressed the way a particular pastor saw his role these were they. He would lead by example but would not be content that he should shoulder all the responsibility himself. It was important for the growth of the church that others should be involved. The Forward Movement may not have been formally constituted, but its spirit certainly lived in the church.

A vital element in Willie's life for many years was the annual holiday. There were two kinds of holiday the Simpsons would take, each fulfilling its own function. On several occasions they took a church party of twenty or so people to places such as Northern Ireland, the Channel Islands, the Isle of Wight or even to foreign lands such as Switzerland. In doing so this fostered fellowship and provided a new slant in mutual perceptions. They visited Carrickfergus in Ulster on two occasions. The hotel they stayed in laid on a programme of sightseeing visits - to White Head, the Giant's Causeway, the Glens of Antrim, to Portrush and the Mountains of Mourn. There was also a holiday in Dublin with tours to 'Killarney and everywhere.' They visited Grindelwald in the Bernese Oberland with a church party. The cable car ride above Grindelwald has remained in Willie's imagination for many years.

Willie and Ida's own annual holiday served a number of purposes, some familiar to anyone in a position of service in the community. If you are available to the people, as Willie insisted he must be, for all waking hours, and even sleeping hours, then there must come the time when a rest is imperative. The only means of such a rest is for the person to be inaccessible. A journey to distant parts ensured this. This also gave the opportunity for man and wife not to have to share their partner with others. Willie's taste for travel was stimulated by Rev. Hedgman in Nottingham as a student - the first opportunity to see for himself the wonders of a great city. As he did as a young man he undertook that task assiduously in the planning and the execution. He read carefully beforehand about what there was to see, what there was about it that made it notable, how it could be reached, where it fitted in the sequence of sights to be seen, and then he ensured that his visiting list was assiduously achieved.

These were lifelong habits - careful, methodical preparation, enthusiastic absorption in the task at hand, but the journeys abroad seem to have tapped this vein in him especially well. Ida seems to have shared this love of detailed planning. Thus they were able to get double value from their holiday, spending evenings reading and planning, anticipating, doing what Willie has always done - looking forward. The choice of venue for their holiday would be made perhaps a year in advance, possibly more. Then they would set about informing themselves of what they would be able to see and how they would get to the places, and particularly the cheapest way of getting to them. He still celebrates the bargain he managed in the transport to Pompeii when they visited Naples by cruise liner. They found their own taxi, knew the way by an alternative route and paid less than half the price paid by the uninformed on board the ship.

Apart from Italy they visited the Holy Land, (this had been as their honeymoon proper during the first year of their marriage), Greek Islands, the Tirol, Madeira, Norway and France, the more distant destinations by sea, others by either road or rail. Some passengers on board the ship became aware that they had among them a very well informed guide. Willie's memory for little anecdotes, for the special place he had read about, not necessarily in Baedeker, was remarkable. The significance of many places for him naturally arose because 'they were a sermon in themselves.' The font in the cathedral of Rouen shows the building reflected in all its glory in the surface of the water in a manner not possible from any other vantage point. He would wander off alone in the search of little treasures which he knew of. In Florence he found the operational centre of the Misericorda, the order which provided an ambulance service for the sick and injured. A roomful of men clad in long cloaks with hoods sat waiting to be summoned to the next place of need.

How did a humble and lowly paid free church pastor afford such holidays? His stipend in the late fifties was still no more than £300 per annum. The answer is by frugal living expenses and the judicious use of investment of savings and capital. During the thirties shipping lines, because of a dearth of trade offered real bargains in cruises. It was possible to go on a three-week cruise round to the Mediterranean 'for a pound a day'.

In 1959 Harry, Willie's brother, six years his senior, had been taken into hospital in Manchester. Willie visited him every week, making the complicated journey from Blakenall to Withington Hospital in Manchester by an assortment of train and bus. At the time he was very familiar with illness, with its symptoms and implications in his role of chaplain in Walsall. Harry remained in hospital for three months and Willie was perplexed about the evident lack of recovery. He described his brother's appearance and symptoms to one of the ward sisters at Manor Hospital. She knew immediately that Harry was suffering from a terminal cancer and said that she was surprised that Willie, of all people, given his great experience as a chaplain, should not have been able to identify his brother's illness. He was surprised himself, but acknowledged that you can be too close to someone. Harry died soon afterwards.

He recalls one journey he made to see Harry in hospital. He left Blakenall on a foggy day in mid-morning to travel to Cannock by bus, some eight miles away. From there he caught another bus to Macclesfield in Cheshire, fifty or so miles, thence to Stockport to the south of Manchester by train. From Stockport he went to the hospital by another bus. Each leg of the journey was delayed by dense fog. So Willie arrived at his brother's bedside after four in the afternoon and was able to stay only a short while before embarking on an equally arduous return journey. He arrived home after two in the morning. He had not even got into bed when there came a knock at the door. To fulfil a long-held promise he was asked to come and lay out a person who had just died. He got to bed at four.

In the early sixties the Congregational churches at Blakenall and at Ryecroft were flourishing. Ryecroft had added an extension to its building which became its Sunday School. Both churches maintained the busy round of activities and duties which had become their hallmark under Willie's care. In effect the duties and obligations of one thriving church had been duplicated by another. In 1964 Willie was sixty-six years old and Ida some three years younger. They were becoming aware of diminishing energies. Willie had promised (probably more to himself than others) that he would not leave until he had seen the Ryecroft extension into being. It was, indeed, built before his time as pastor was concluded.

So, there was the prospect of retirement. In the late thirties Willie's brother, Harry, had built a pair of semi-detached, stone houses in New Road, Buxworth. Buxworth is two miles west of Chinley down the valley. The houses were, in true Simpson fashion, solid and simple, with good living space, three-bedroomed and on a site that fell away from the road. This gave space for a good 'working' cellar and garage under the house. One of the pair had been set aside for Willie and Ida to retire to when the need arose. They would not own the house but it had been left in trust in Harry's will for Willie and Ida for as long as either should live or for as long as either should need it. He would be able to return to his place of birth and live among his own people. The prospect, especially to Ida, with a release from the daily round of duty, must have been enticing. Willie, on the other hand, must have wondered about the idea of having time on his hands. He may have been at retirement age (in fact when he left Blakenall he was sixty-seven) but his appetite for work and his energy, though less than it had been, were of a man much younger.

The house at Buxworth had been occupied for a year or so by the then current Minister at Chinley Chapel, Rev. G. A. Thomas. The Trustees of the Chapel had decided to sell their old manse under the viaduct in Chapel Milton and build a new one. The financial burden of a full-time minister, the expense of a new manse and the purchase and maintenance of a car for the minister's use was becoming too much for the dwindling congregation of Chinley Chapel to support. Then in July, 1964 Rev. Thomas said that he would be taking up a new pastorate in North Wales and discussions began among the Trustees as to a replacement. Willie was becoming aware towards the end of the year that the financial state of Chinley Chapel was becoming increasingly precarious. He told Ida that 'there was something seriously amiss there' and suggested that it would be helpful if he could offer his services as minister on a temporary basis. Ida thought they were going to retire. But she knew her husband and she knew what her own calling was and that she would follow Willie wherever providence took him. So the wheels were in motion which were to take Willie back to Chinley Chapel as Minister. It was not to be an entirely smooth process. The account of how it was to be accomplished belongs in the next chapter.

There were crucial differences in attitude and feeling between Willie and Ida in their contemplation of the end of the Blakenall ministry. He could look back on his work there with great satisfaction and pleasure, as indeed could Ida, but he knew the church and the community he was going to intimately. She had never lived in Chinley. She had visited Willie's mother there and had been with Willie in the Chapel when he was a visiting preacher. They had been married in the chapel. Nevertheless, Ida believed that after the end of the Blakenall ministry they would retire. Beyond that, I suspect that she was not quite as forward-looking as Willie. No-one could be! So Ida would feel regrets about leaving Blakenall and Ryecroft more than Willie. This he acknowledged. He spoke of her great sadness on the day that they left, but it did not deter him. He was utterly convinced of the rightness of what was to come next. He was contemplating another real job, something else to get his teeth into.

Which of his five ministries had been the most enjoyable? This was a question which occurred more than once. Willie would never commit himself to a direct answer. Was he being diplomatic, avoiding hurting the feelings of those he had enjoyed less? Or could he not genuinely distinguish between them? Certainly the pleasures and challenges were different in each community, though basically the challenges were met by him in each instance in a characteristically Simpson way - by determined and energetic work. Two of the communities were the ground where such work gave him his greatest reward. The first was Mexborough where his energy was at its zenith. The second was Blakenall which I believe was his heyday. It was his heyday because he had both the energy and the benefit of experience, and because he was among the kind of folk he understood and who understood him. Most of all, it was because he had a wife who extended and complemented his ministry, who tempered his ideas, whose judgment he valued implicitly and together with whom he had suffered.

The people said, 'We've got two ministers!' A reporter who was interviewing Willie at the gathering on their departure from Blakenall asked him about his hobbies. A man nearby overheard the question. 'He doesn't have any. His hobby is people!' he said with great conviction. The memories of Willie Simpson from Mexborough and Enderby are affectionate, but they do not have quite the same tenderness as that seen in the people of Blakenall.

9

Coming Home

For Willie, coming home to Chinley to become minister of Chinley Independent Chapel was a fulfilment. It was fulfilment of an ambition, if it can be argued that he had any ambition at all. His view is that 'You do not have an ambition when you have a vocation for the ministry.' When he set off on the road to the ministry it could not be stated that the single, ultimate goal was to become minister of Chinley Chapel. But he must have entertained the idea more than once when he paid his regular visits to the area to see his mother. During these visits he would generally walk up from Chinley to visit 'Arthur's grave'. (The grave of his ancestors.) Simply being in the church yard on such occasions was a great joy to him. It was such a hallowed place for him that he even went as far as to suggest that burial in Chinley Chapel graveyard meant automatic entry to heaven. On the other hand he was far too committed and too busy in his successive ministries to have any distracting preoccupation with the pastorate of Chinley Chapel.

However, when he did come home to Chinley, it called to mind May

Birchenough's prophetic words when he had ventured into the pulpit as a boy, 'You'll be up there proper one day, Willie.' In fact he had preached from that pulpit on a number of occasions even before he was ordained. He began before he went to college, as one of the requirements of college acceptance was that his own church should have heard him preach. In Willie's mind the real ring of May Birchenough's words said more than that he would merely preach from that pulpit. One day he would be the minister. He also recalled a day when he was twenty when he met a lady in Whitehough. She asked how things were at Chinley Chapel. He told her that everything was going well, upon which she said, simply, 'The day will come when you will be minister of Chinley Chapel.' He never knew why she chose to say this.

Coming home to Chinley Chapel was a fulfilment also in that it was the granting of a heart's desire. Throughout his long ministry, though he had always given his entire mind and energy to the task in hand, as he described it himself, 'There was always the hankering to go back to Chinley Chapel.' To be able to give his energy and his time to the daily concerns of this beloved place was almost beyond his imaginings. To be able to conduct services and offer prayer and thanksgiving to God from within his 'blessed sanctuary' on a regular basis was a source of real joy. Furthermore he would be carrying out his ministry well and truly among his own folk, which for Willie was the crowning joy.

In retrospect, the opportunity for him to come to Chinley Chapel was propitious for both church and minister. The retirement from Blakenall was, in the final analysis, determined by the emergence of the vacancy at Chinley Chapel. Ida believed (and no doubt hoped) that retirement was in the offing, if not imminent. What would have happened had the vacancy at Chinley not arisen? Would they have retired? 'We should have just gone on,' he said, presumably until the vacancy did occur. The intention to retire might have been mooted for some time before the notion of taking on Chinley emerged into broad daylight. But the notion of Chinley had been in gestation for a long time, possibly since he was sixteen years of age. It could be that Willie's conception of 'retirement' was different from Ida's. Whereas she would see it as a shedding of all the duties of formal ministry, in his mind it meant no more than a lightening of the load of the daily round of a busy, young and active church such as Blakenall. 'It'll be like a retirement here, not something every night,' he said to Ida. In fact, I do not believe that even this or any other notion of retirement was in his mind. The central, uncomplicated impulse was to return to Chinley Chapel as minister and thereby to round off a life in the ministry. In the light of how mutual needs, of church and minister, were met, this was yet another example of how providence and the Simpsons worked hand in hand.

'You'll be up there proper one day, Willie.'

So it was not entirely co-incidental that Willie became available just at the time that the church needed a minister. However, the element of co-incidence, providence, call it what you will, lay in the fact that a church in need of a minister, but without the means to pay for one, was put into contact with the minister in need of this church. What is more, this was the minister who was prepared to work for next to nothing simply to be there, which was no small consideration. Furthermore, he knew, if only from the very dearth of information coming out of the people he communicated with in Chinley, notably James Price (the treasurer and a son of Rev. D. J. Price) that things were not right. He had other, more tangible evidence from his own business and property concerns in the district. He recalls sitting by the fire in the manse at Blakenall. 'I said to Ida, "There's something badly amiss at Chinley Chapel. I must write to James Price and offer my help."'

To elaborate on this from the church's point of view; on the departure of Rev. G. A. Thomas, first intimated in July 1964, the chapel trustees began a dialogue with the Moderator of the Congregational Union (as it then was) as to the possibility of a joint pastorate with Whaley Bridge Congregational Church. The trustees wanted to continue with a minister of their own, not one who was shared with another church. But this was by no means a viable proposition given the dire state of the chapel's finances at the time. Basically, the equation of the income from a small congregation and the expenditure to maintain a place of worship and a sole minister was out of balance and growing steadily worse. The chapel and the grounds were in need of considerable attention. The Sunday School building was a burden in many respects. There had been the expense of building a new manse, the original one under the viaduct in Chapel Milton having too many disadvantages associated with its age (it was a late-eighteenth century building) to be a comfortable home for the minister and his family. (Willie thinks of it as 'off the beaten track and with a lonely and difficult approach for visitors.') The minister's stipend and pastoral expenses, specifically his use of a car to get about a rural area, in the context of all the outgoings, were too much for the church finances to bear. James Price was 'at his wits'end' about the seemingly unstoppable decline.

The dialogue with the moderator about a joint pastorate, which would have been the first in Chinley Chapel's history, was continued throughout the autumn of 1964 and into early 1965. The congregation was consulted, enquiries were made about how it would be expected to work and then in February, 1965, the impression is, reluctantly and with a heavy heart, approaches were made to Whaley Bridge Deacons. At this point a letter was received by the trustees from Rev. Simpson enquiring about the vacant pastorate. The trustees then met him but decided that nevertheless they would accept an invitation to meet the Whaley Bridge Deacons. Options were being kept open. The trustees' minutes for 29th March 1965 record the decision to call a church meeting on 4th April to find the congregation's views on a joint pastorate.

There were several bodies of opinion about what the best course of action would be. There were those who felt that anything but a joint pastorate would be suitable. There were those who did not know Rev. Simpson and who were very doubtful about taking on a man who was aged sixty-seven and retiring from his previous church. Surely this was a man of much diminished energy and possibly out-of-date attitudes? How would he contend with a youth group which, though it was from a semi-rural backwater, knew that out there was the Swinging Sixties. Members of the church had seen him conduct the funeral of Edmund Bradbury, who had died in November, 1963. Edmund was revered by Willie as a lifelong friend and a descendant of the Bradbury family of Coldwell Clough on Kinder, the son of Samuel Bradbury (Willie's 'saintly man') who was Chairman of Chinley Chapel Trustees in Willie's boyhood. But Edmund had not maintained the family's close connection with the chapel. Because of this the manner and content of Willie's funeral eulogy of Edmund had caused a degree of perplexity among some of the members. This caused some uncertainty about the prospect of him as minister. There were others who did not know him but who felt that, given the state of church finances, it should not look a gift horse in the mouth. Perhaps their feelings were not so strong as to say that Willie was any port in the storm, but he was better than no minister. There were those, very few in number, who had a long memory of how he had risen from the ranks, ranks to which they had belonged themselves, and who resented Willie's assumption of a place of distinction among them. There were those who simply did not know. And finally, there were those who knew him of old and were enthusiastic and determined advocates of taking him on.

In answer to the doubters, particularly on the score of his age and energy, Willie's chief advocates, among them Ellis Barnes, George Simpson, and Frank Nadin, stated their unequivocal confidence in the man. It was suggested that if it came to a running race, or working the fields or some such task, this new man could give men much younger than his years a good start. They followed their instincts and pleaded irresistibly for him to be taken on. Being trustees they knew in detail what a parlous state the church was in financially. There were debts which, so long as there had been a minister on full stipend they could not see any hope of settling. In fact, the prospect was of worse. Even without a minister, in the interregnum, there seemed to be no hope of setting things to rights. So, to the likes of Ellis Barnes the arrival of Willie Simpson was a gift from above. Not only would they have a minister, but he would be a worker, he would be full time, solely attached to Chinley Chapel and he would hardly be an expense. Nor would he need any time to acclimatise. 'Come and live with us in the manse, Willie, you're one of us!' He knew the district intimately, its geography and its people.

When the decision to give Willie the Call came it came quickly and was given a momentum which took some by surprise. It was not unanimous and there are those now who remember their own reservations at the time. Nearly all of them, though, are prepared to say that they were soon reassured that their hesitancy was unjustified. For Willie the Call had none of the stuffiness and formality which surrounds the invitation to take on some ministries. It was more like the family taking in a long lost son. It was a genuine welcome home. James Price's formal letter of invitaion, dated 3rd June 1965, said

> *'The Church Meeting last night unanimously recommended the Trustees to invite you to our vacant pastorate and become our Minister. The Trustees are very pleased indeed to carry out this recommendation, and would like to express their heartfelt gratitude to you for the kind offer to assist us in any way we thought proper.*
> *We all hope that your ministry with us will be a rewarding one and that you and your wife will be very happy amongst us.'*

Willie's sermon for his first service on his return was on 'Building Bridges'. This is a metaphor with many applications. For Willie himself he was rebuilding a bridge with his own past. For Ida the bridge she needed was the means of establishing contact with a community which was not part of her as it was of her husband. On the other hand Willie knew that he had to establish himself again among a new generation of Chinley Chapel folk, many of whom knew little of him. There was a bridge to build. The church itself had reached a point in its history when it had appeared that its very existence was in doubt. It could now take a first tentative step to cross a bridge it thought had disappeared. Also, of course, he was the bridge himself between those trustees who had taken the responsibility for giving him the Call and the members of the congregation for whom he was an unknown quantity. Chinley Chapel is physically situated in the shadow of two viaducts and a railway bridge

Leaving Blakenall, for Ida, was distressing. 'She was in tears for the whole day on the previous Sunday and she was not a person to be in tears,' Willie recalls. Eighteen years of service and deep involvement in the lives of the folk they loved was not to be lightly released. The original intention had been to retire to the house set aside for them in New Road, Buxworth, which had been occupied for three years by the Thomas family while the question of a site for the new manse was settled and the building of it accomplished. Now the Simpsons were moving to a different house, a manse, with a new set of responsibilities and obligations in a new ministry. They were not the pastures new that were envisaged initially. In their sixties there was to be a new commitment to work.

They moved to Chinley on a Saturday in early July, 1965. Willie stayed for the afternoon in Blakenall to conduct a wedding service, working till the end. Ida went over to Chinley to direct the setting up of the new home. When the furniture arrived George Simpson, Frank Nadin and the immediate neighbour, the caretaker of the nearby Council offices, John Gregory and his wife, who were to become staunch friends of the Simpsons, set to work with a will to install the new minister and his wife. When Willie arrived later in John Biddulph's car with 'all the cut glass' he was able to walk into an established home.

The next morning they went into the chapel for morning service and Willie preached for the first time as minister. Then after the service Ida and he stood together at the church door to wish the congregation good morning and to introduce themselves. Willie remembers this occasion as having such warmth that it restored Ida after the trauma of the previous Sunday. Certainly, for Willie it was an occasion of some euphoria - 'absolutely marvellous, my beloved Chinley!' I suppose that Ida was able to deal with the occasion in the characteristic, calm, phlegmatic way which was her nature and a function of her age at the time. She may have felt sorrow at having to leave Blakenall but she knew that the call given to her husband was an essential part of her own calling. Very quickly she won the hearts and the great respect of the people of Chinley. She soon became the integral part of the Simpson ministry that she had been throughout their lives together. From the many Chinley people I have spoken to I have never heard a solitary word of anything but affection and respect for her.

In the evening of that first Sunday back in Chinley Willie went to preach at Thornsett Church, which is over the hill between New Mills and Hayfield. This was a long-standing commitment which he would not break. So Roy Booth came to act as supply at Chinley Chapel, resonances of Mexborough and Blakenall for the Simpsons.

'Everywhere was a legacy of dilapidation,' said Willie about Chinley Chapel on his arrival. 'The church, the vestry, the Sunday School, the graveyard, the walls, all needed attention. There was woodworm in the pews. The kitchen in the Sunday School was in a mess. There was no heating in there. On Sunday it was like an ice house. I would go over before breakfast on a Sunday morning to light fires and warm the place up. And there was a debt for a thousand pounds. We owed five hundred to the county union.'

It was just the kind of challenge to suit him. Instinctively he began setting targets. The vestry was his first priority. He decided that it must be tidied up and re-decorated so that 'you could ask anyone in there and not be ashamed.' The heating problem in the Sunday School was tackled later, in 1966, when he heard that Hadfield's had 'a heating apparatus' (a boiler), as Willie named it, that they were discarding. He advised that they approach Tom Hadfield, one of the descendants of J. J. ('He had thousands and he loved bread and jam.') The trick with a Hadfield if you wanted money from them was, as Willie's mentor, Rev. Edmondson, had advised, to 'mention the father'. 'I shouldn't have come to you if your father had been with us,' said Willie. 'George

Simpson told Tom Hadfield how I would go and light the fires in the Sunday School early on a Sunday morning. Tom was sorry for the children being cold.' So the 'heating apparatus' was duly obtained as a gift and winter in the Sunday School became more bearable.

The chapel's debt was paid off by the last day of November, 1965. James Price died suddenly in his late fifties only nine months after Willie's arrival but he lived to see the chapel become solvent again. From the moment Willie came back to Chinley there were clear signs of recovery and James Price must have felt the burden easing. There is a tribute to James in the Trustees' minutes, an appreciation of a concerned and conscientious man.

'I don't how it is. Money follows me,' Willie said again. 'People would come up to me when I was in the churchyard and say, "We're glad to see you back, Willie! Here, take this." And they would give five pounds or ten pounds.' Of course, there were other sources from which money followed him, sources from which the money was encouraged to follow. And once someone had made a contribution he or she would be encouraged to follow the precedent on one or other of the Special Occasions which soon became part of the church calendar.

His intimate knowledge of the district was no disadvantage in finding sources of help. He knew who had money and who would be prepared to help, if only for old time's sake. Furthermore, as some have remarked, 'He was prepared to do the leg work to contact them.' And 'leg work' it was, because he was still riding his bicycle and still prepared to walk about to make his calls. He also put his knowledge of and acquaintance with local tradesmen, builders, dry-stone wallers, to good effect. Their services were every bit as valuable as any money that others could give. He was prepared to labour himself for the skilled man, William ('Bill') Noblett, in the reconstruction and repair of stone walls around the churchyard. (Ellis Barnes told me that 'Bill only charged £50 for the whole job'.) Here was the evidence for the doubters that this was no ordinary sixty-seven-year-old. He was soon immersed in the business of restoring the fabric of the church property to the state which he felt to be right and proper. The first task he saw was the restoration of self-respect for the church body. Standards had been allowed to slip. There was no explicit policy in getting the people to work together. He simply followed his instincts.

When Willie became minister of Chinley Chapel there was a small congregation for Sunday services, probably no more than about twenty people except on special occasions. The Sunday School at this time was under the leadership of Joy Needham. She had been Sunday School Superintendent for a relatively short period. There were about ten children. Willie and Joy got on well immediately. He admired her ability as a teacher, her facility for gaining and holding the children's attention without any apparent effort. She had a beautifully modulated voice, was very musical and had presence in the schoolroom. She was young, bringing up her own young family at the time and committed to her Christian work. Willie was prepared to leave the teaching and the leadership to Joy. She gave the teaching some focus by entering the children for scripture examinations. He saw his own role to be in finding children to come to Sunday School, and thus to see to the future of the church. So, if for some reason he learned of children living at a particular house, perhaps because the family had had a child baptised in the church or because they were newly arrived in the district, he arrived at the door with an inimitable gentle, hat-raising enquiry for children for Chinley Chapel Sunday School.

Some believe all his 'leg work' in the district was solely in the pursuit of funds and only to visit those houses where he knew he would find them. Others, among them Joy Needham, knew that the growth of the Sunday School over the years of Willie's incumbency was, in great measure, due to his own missionary work. As the numbers in the school grew he and Joy decided that they would hold a party when they achieved twenty-five children. The party duly took place. Then there was another party when they reached fifty children. They eventually reached sixty-five on the Sunday School roll, remarkable for a church in its relatively isolated position. The church's strength in both numbers and fellowship in the nineteen eighties and nineties had its roots in these times. There is no means of establishing how many members of the school of the sixties and seventies either remained or returned to become adult members of the church. It is reasonable to surmise that the identifiable spirit and reputation of the church was re-established in the local community at this time. People, particularly newcomers who were coming to inhabit the newly built houses which were appearing around Chinley and Chapel-en-le-Frith, became aware of the existence of the church, if not for themselves to attend as regular worshippers, then at least as a place to send their children to. Chinley Chapel was re-appearing on the local map. Once more the Simpson persona had an important part to play.

The folk of the district are often very surprised that Willie has survived for so long. They do not question his health or vitality, or indeed his habit of confronting anyone. His health has always been robust. In fact, they refer to his means of getting about. He rode his bicycle until he was seventy. Then he suffered a broken leg when he was knocked down by a car by the gateway to the High Peak Council Offices which are thirty yards or so from the manse. This was a blessing in disguise because he was becoming less adept on the bicycle and increasingly less aware of the growing traffic.

While his leg was broken he did not miss a service. He preached from below the pulpit, sitting in a wheelchair with his leg sticking out in front of him. 'Children used to touch the plaster as they walked past,' he said. 'Ernest Winterbottom from Stoddart Hall used to push me in the wheelchair. He were a big, 'efty man. I would say, "Ernest, tha' munna topple me o'er!" And he would say, "I shallna topple thee o'er. No need t'worry."' Willie conducted wedding ceremonies sitting on the communion table. The register was signed in church. 'I am going to make it possible for you to see the bride and bridegroom sign the register. It will be rather nice for them and for you.' ('Mother always said, "Willie'll find a way out!"'). When the plaster was removed from his leg he was determined to get his mobility back to normal (Ernest Winterbottom provided some liniment when the plaster came off by way of restoring flexibility to the leg, liniment which he used on his farm horse. 'If it's good enough for th'orse, it's good enough for t'parson.'). Willie applied himself assiduously, and noisily, to the physiotherapy sessions. He was quite prepared to put up with the pain and discomfort of getting his limb working again so long as he could shout and groan about it. He says that the physiotherapist said they had never had such a noisy patient. He was warned that he would have arthritic problems in his leg as he got older, but he says he is still waiting for signs of the arthritis.

Having had to forsake the bicycle Willie has become more dependent on the generosity of car-owners. As I have said before, for longer distances he was always prepared to hint to, cajole, suggest to, occasionally even confront, friends for conveyance to a variety of destinations. A fund of lifts became available. Many of us have taken him to hospitals, nursing homes, sheltered housing and people's homes 'to visit the old people'. It was no duty. The conversation always flows, there is humour and a sharp awareness of what is happening on the journey. When I left him at a hospital he stood on the footpath leading to the entrance until I drove off, the innate courtesy seeing me safely on my way. Then I saw him in the driving mirror carefully taking his bearings and then directing his characteristic, scurrying gait towards the hospital ward. I returned to collect him at the appointed time. He never kept me waiting and I felt that I must not keep him waiting. We travelled home together exchanging our experiences and then he would tell me how much I had shared in his ministry for the afternoon. Finally, before he left the car, off would come his hat, my hand would be grasped lightly but firmly and there would be a prayer of thanksgiving for the joint ministry, and his friend would be committed to God's care 'as he homeward goes.'

Willie's ability to get about the country without his own means of transport is legendary. There are many examples of a decision to go to visit people in places far and near and of setting off without the slightest notion of how the journey was to be accomplished. He would simply announce that he was going and, on being asked how he intended to get there, would reply, 'The Lord will provide!' He walked out of the house and hailed the first vehicle coming along, stepping into the road almost recklessly, with dog-collar very visible. Almost invariably he would be given a lift. Again, the Lord did provide, and preserved him from the injury that many have said he has been 'lucky' to avoid.

For three months after they had left Blakenall he went back for one day a week to fulfil his chaplaincy duties at the hospital and to watch over the building work which was still in progress to provide the Sunday School at Ryecroft church. He conducted funerals and even one wedding on some of these days, and regularly relied on hitch-hiking. On the way home he would be taken by John Biddulph to a strategic point on the journey where he knew he could expect transport, the road for Ashbourne north of Lichfield. In his own words:

'Then up comes one of Sam Longson's lorries' (Sam owned the large transport business in Chapel-en-le-Frith. He was almost a contemporary of Willie, someone he had known since boyhood.) 'I stopped him. I said, "Can you give me a lift to Chapel-en-le-Frith?"

"No! I'm forbidden."

'I said, "If Sam knew I were 'ere - and stranded, and you'd left me on the road - he would be very sorry."

"Get in."

'I said, "When you get back, tell 'im, straight away, that you've given Willie Simpson a lift on the road. He'll not give you the sack."

'When Sam became ill and I visited him, I told him about this lift. I said, "You know, Sam, I was grateful to you that day. It was getting towards eventide and for the life of me I didn't know how I was going to get home."'

One evening in the summer of 1969 he said to Ida, 'I must go and see Mr. Biddulph tomorrow.' (John's father who was ill in the general hospital in Wolverhampton). He woke up next morning undecided as to whether he should go.

'I went across to the chapel. Why I should go across to the chapel I don't know. But I came back. I didn't do anything at the chapel, I just went across and came back. I said, "I'm going." My wife said, "Well however in the world you are going to get to Wolverhampton I don't know." I said, "The Lord'll provide if necessary."

'I got out on the road and the first car that came along stopped. "Well," I said, "are you going to Buxton?"

"Yes," he said. "Are you?"

I said, "I am."

"Do you want a lift?"

I said, "Yes, please." When we got to the bottom of Spring Gardens in Buxton I said, "I'm going to Wolverhampton."

He said, "So am I!" (The chances that his 'lift' should be going to exactly the place he needed to go to were remote, to say the least, given the two ends of his journey.) 'So, of course that meant I stayed in the car and we arrived at Wolverhampton. I didn't know where the General Hospital was. He was going to the eye hospital. The first person I met on stepping out of the car was a lady from whom I asked for directions as to the hospital.

'She said, "I'm a nurse there. Who are you going to visit?"

"I'm going to visit Mr. Biddulph."

"I'm nursing him!"

'I said, "Well then, I'll entrust myself to you." We got to the hospital and she said to the lady in charge, "This gentleman's come from Chinley." And in ten minutes there was a lovely dinner for me. And then I stayed the afternoon with Mr. Biddulph. His wife came later and then I went home with her and stayed the night.

'Next morning John brought me from Wolverhampton to the familiar turn for Ashbourne out of Lichfield. He had to leave me because he had to go to his job as a schoolteacher. I said, "I'll be all right here because every car from here will be going to Buxton." The first car that came along I was in it, and I was on my way before John had got off. When I asked the driver how far he was going he said, "I'm going to Glossop." "Oh," I said, "you'll pass my door!"

'Then, I said, "I'm a Congregational minister."

'He said, "I'm a deacon in a Congregational church!"

'I thought, "How wonderfully God has provided for my visit! I was home by twenty to ten in the morning. And when I told my wife the story she were amazed."

After John Biddulph's marriage some years earlier, Ida and Willie were brought home by John's father by motor-bike and sidecar from the Midlands back to Chinley. There is an abiding vision of this immaculately clad, elegant, elderly lady in the confines of a sidecar, with her husband in his clerical garb riding pillion beside her. Was Willie aware of the picture they cut? Probably he was not entirely unaware. While the journey by motor-bike would serve its own very practical (and economical) purpose, he would be somewhat aware of the image they presented and would, in fact, actively enjoy their prominence. He certainly enjoyed the experience of travelling by motor-bike. What Ida thought and felt I do not know. One impression is that she would follow Willie wherever he chose to go. Another impression is of a more retiring nature than Willie's. She would not have revelled in the journey quite as much as he did. Appearances did matter. The importance she attached to good, well-cut clothes are a clear indication of this. But I can imagine a degree of impish amusement in them both as they bowled along. 'Weren't you cold?' 'Oh, no, it was July, a beautiful July day.' he replied.

As I have said, Willie's instinct was always to look for a means of securing the future of his church. In this regard his focus tended to be the practical rather than the spiritual. He took very seriously the brief of the original trustees of Chinley Chapel, to maintain a place of worship on the land set aside for the purpose in 1711. Any neglect which put the building in jeopardy was a betrayal of the original trust. Likewise, the Sunday School, the future of the church, needed maintenance and fostering as a building and as an institution. It was not enough simply to keep the building going. It was important to give it modern comforts, so long as they did not alter the essential character of the building. He has no wish to make a penance of religious observance. We should be joyful, and warm and comfortable, in our praise. So, during his time at Chinley Chapel central heating was installed in the church and in the Sunday School. The Sunday School ceiling was lowered so that the heat did not escape into the roof space. The work of the woodworm was halted and wood restored. The organ was rescued (in one respect, mice were the culprits). Stonework, roofs, guttering were all given attention, painting and decorating was carried out, all achieved against a background of a steady strengthening of the church's finances, having paid off debts within six months of his arrival. The work was not achieved overnight. He began a process which continued after his departure twelve years later. The vital effect he had in the first instance was in restoring a belief in the future in people whose hearts were sinking fast, with a refreshing draught of Simpson optimism - and faith.

At first Willie was prepared to accept only a nominal stipend from Chinley Chapel, no more than £5 a week. When he felt that the church's financial base was becoming strong enough he asked the Trustees to establish a fund into which they paid the monies he would have received had he been paid a full stipend. The object was to create a fund which would secure for the church its own minister for the foreseable future after the end of his own pastorate. Throughout his period of office there is a record in the Trustees' minutes of varying amounts being placed from time to time in this Trust Fund. By the time the Simpsons left the church there was enough to ensure that it could always aspire to having its own minister. It would not be enough to resist the effects of high inflation, but the existence of the fund had done what the tackling of the decline in the fabric of the church had done. It was tangible evidence of re-discovered self-belief.

Also there began to happen what had happened in Willie's other churches. When people made their wills they came to him for advice and asked what he felt they should leave for the church. His answer would always be non-committal. He would let the inquirer provide the answer. People knew their own circumstances better than he did. They knew what their families might expect. But frequently the question would be, 'How much must I leave to make sure that my shilling (or whatever amount) can go into the collection every week after I'm gone?' There he would give explicit advice.

Some years later the church was surprised, as Willie himself was, to learn of large bequests, amounts well in excess of the fund that had been created from his 'stipend'. These bequests must have had something to do with Willie's presence in the church. In Willie's mind they became sacrosanct. He felt that the church should not forget the original intention behind them - to maintain the memory of those who had left the money, in the weekly offertory. So, years later after he had left Chinley Chapel when the church was contemplating large capital projects such as the building of a car park he disapproved of the wish to use the capital funds for such purposes. He felt acutely the dilution of the intentions of those who had come to him for advice, even a betrayal of their trust. He also felt that to touch these funds was to put a hard-won future once more in jeopardy. Nevertheless, when for example, the car park did come into being and he saw what an enormous advantage it provided, both in terms of road safety and, especially, the enhanced approach to the chapel for worshippers, by the path through the churchyard, he acknowledged the benefit generously. He was too practical to fail to see such an advantage, and would feel that if the money had had to be laid out, at least it was well spent. He would also be well aware that had it not been for his own efforts on his return to Chinley there would be no question whatsoever that the church could contemplate a car park or anything else. Willie could not really have been surprised that funds began to 'appear'. Providence, money and the Simpsons somehow always seemed to work together.

The establishment of the Trust Fund raised a number of issues among the Trustees at the time of Willie's pastorate. Retrospectively, having started the process of providing a much more secure financial base for the church caused some tensions and heart-searching among church members twenty-five years later. The first issue between some Trustees and Willie was 'Whose fund is it?' This came about because there were times when needs for money arose and the only visible source at the time was the fund. No one wished to use the capital, but it was felt that to use the interest was reasonable. This was entirely counter to Willie's conception of the fund, and his argument was that the monies were in fact being set aside by him. The contrary argument was that had this been so there would have been a liability for income tax. I do not know whether it ever became finally necessary to dip into the fund. I suspect that it was not. Some Trustees, not to mention Willie himself, would go a long way to avoid such a necessity. All of this speaks of their loyalty to him and of their own determination that now that church fortunes had been turned round they should never again be allowed to reach the dire state of affairs prevailing when Willie first arrived. The argument about the fund rumbled on for several years, the need to use it diminishing as the church grew stronger, while, ironically, the fund itself grew bigger. It did serve one very important purpose, in that it forced the drawing up of a new trust deed which rationalised and clarified the duties and obligations of the Trustees and ensured, to Willie's satisfaction, that any decision to use the fund, in part or whole, had to be with the unanimous consent of the Trustees.

The heart-searching mentioned is a familiar issue for some churches. No doubt there are churches who would be glad of the dilemma I am about to describe. Their daily need is practical survival to keep heart and soul and, usually, the church building together, though in the face of their unremitting fight, can they ever be described as 'weak'? The dilemma for a 'well-off' church concerns the extent to which the focus of a church's energies should be its own comfort. Is there not a danger that in the determination to use mere human striving, planning and contriving to sustain one's own church community that the greater needs of others in the ever-widening circle of human need slip from notice? Those members of Chinley Chapel who remember acutely what Willie came to in 1965 reply that that is indeed a concern, but there is no use in being in the situation where there is no church community left to show any concern for others, and to be in the position of not being able to do anything about it. They would certainly see little value in the argument that the strongest church is the most impecunious one.

It is not charitable to Willie to take the view that one of his legacies to Chinley Chapel is an over-concern with its own financial security. That judgment takes no account of the affection that the folk of Chinley Chapel and the district had for him and Ida. Nor does it recognise that another way in which he went about securing the future was in the best way possible; by finding children for the Sunday School. Nevertheless some felt that the focus at the time of Willie's pastorate was too much on money, even at the expense of the spiritual. They recall that there was virtually no formally organised Bible study during his pastorate. This was an omission not least in that it was remarked upon. People felt the need and the need was not met. It could be seen as a lost opportunity for Willie, given his intimate knowledge of scripture. On the other hand account must be taken of the spirituality of Willie's mission among the people, whose houses he would visit in concern for their welfare.

Above all else the Simpsons were accessible. The symbol of this accessibility was the tea tray which was always ready on the sitting-room table in the manse, fine china cups and saucers on a pristine tray cloth. The image is of Ida's smiling welcome for the caller, the sense of time available, the unhurried cup of tea and the essential warmth and calm. Willie was genuinely pleased and welcomed you with warmth when you called, and made a fuss and possibly resorted to the well-worn phrases of welcome. Ida was equally pleased, just as warm, but quieter and giving more space for the caller to settle. Not that Willie lacked a degree of perception with callers, but, by his own admission, he did not have the fine, intuitive judgment that he admired so much in his wife. If either could have been said to have had a domain, then the manse belonged to Ida, the church and the district to Willie.

Within a short time of his return to Chinley Willie instituted a Special Occasion. He called it the 'Gathering of the Golden Years', a title which in itself says a great deal about Willie. Of course, it betrays his penchant for the grandiose. There are echoes of the alliteration which pepper his sermons. But the choice of the word 'gathering' is significant. It implies more than just 'meeting', and is distinct from 'commemorative service' in not having such formality. People gather together without the sense of duty and obligation that a formal meeting can imply. There is warmth and a sense of one's own volition about it. There is also the sense of many and diverse people coming from a variety of directions. These people come from a long line of Golden Years. That was Willie's perception. He looked back on a lifetime in the ministry, doing what he was called to do and thoroughly enjoying it. And now, having come full circle and returned to where he felt he really belonged the years were truly golden.

The Gathering of the Golden Years was held on the anniversary of Willie's ordination, 'on the second or third Saturday in July'. A lot of work and thought would go into the day. People from the district who were not generally able to come to church because of the infirmity of age or because of illness were sought out and a special effort made to bring them. Later, people from all his previous churches were invited. Others, especially those who had well-established family connections with the history of Chinley Chapel, the Bagshawe family, descendants of William in particular, were asked along. Mrs. Bagshawe, the wife of F. E. G. Bagshawe of Snitterton Hall, Matlock, came in spite of her being seriously afflicted with arthritis. The church would be full, regaled in flowers - the years were golden, after all - and there would be a ham tea to follow. And Willie would be dashing around before and after the service determinedly gathering everybody in. 'Visiting ministers were surprised at the number of people we managed to get together on a Saturday afternoon,' said Willie. The purpose behind the day, initially, was to let the people know that Chinley Chapel was alive and well again, a purpose duly fulfilled. Later, in 1975, ten years on, when Willie was still at the chapel serving his 'stop-gap' function, the occasion was used to celebrate the fiftieth anniversary of his ordination in Mexborough. On this occasion their friends, Mary and John Gregory, made an enormous cake, which was a scale model of the chapel. (John had been a builder and so the scale was accurate.) The cake was complete with ivy and the vestry which is a small attached outbuilding at Chinley, and, to Willie's delight, there was a tiny, black-clad figure at the vestry door.

Naturally, the occasion also served to provide a focus for the efforts of church members and, again, it would raise a few more pounds. The organ one year had had to have extensive restoration and repairs, work which had cost £1800. The focus of the Gathering that year was to use the occasion to re-dedicate the restored instrument in the memory of James Price. 'We still needed a hundred pounds at the beginning of the service,' Willie said, 'and do you know there was ninety-nine pounds in the collection. A lady came to me as I stood wishing everyone good afternoon. She said, "I let the offertory box go by because I only had a pound note." I said to her, "That doesn't matter. Come across and have some tea." "No," she said, "I want to give it to you." And so we got the hundred pounds we needed.'

The Price family was an important thread for Willie between the time of his departure for Paton College and his return as minister. Rev. D. J. Price was minister in the twenties and his son, James, was church treasurer until his own death soon after Willie's return. Then James's sister, Beatrice, maintained the family connection to the present day. She was one of the first women to become a Trustee of Chinley Chapel. Until her retirement she had been a long time in a responsible administrative capacity in industry, a lone woman when equality of opportunity was not given even the lip-service it has come to enjoy now. She has had a lifelong love of theatre, especially for comedy and revue and continued to be a regular figure in the productions put on by the Chapel-en-le-Frith Players. She refused to divulge her age, politely but firmly, on the grounds that 'people would have something to say when they saw a woman of my age cavorting on the stage like that.' Willie holds her in great regard. For him her abiding qualities are her strength and her humour. The best compliment he felt he could pay her when she was made a Chapel Trustee was that she was 'like a man, she had the mind of a man, the attitude of a man.' This does less than justice to the particular feminine attributes which Bea has of kindness, warmth and sensitivity, attributes not exclusively feminine, but more often associated with a woman than a man. The point is that in Willie's mind one of the first women to break the Chinley Chapel Trustee mould had to have the strength that he felt was a particularly male facet.

Bea's long connection with the church was an asset. Like the others of similar pedigree she was very aware of the long standing bequests which had been made to sustain specific aspects of church life. One of these was made by Thomas Slacke, who lived at Slacke Hall which is a mile or so out of Chapel-en-le-Frith on the Castleton road. He was a doctor and Justice of the Peace whose life and service are commemorated on a stone plaque in Chinley Chapel. He died in 1878 leaving £2000 in Indian stock which yielded, at 3%, £60 per annum. The stipulation of the bequest was that the interest should be used as follows: £30 for the minister's stipend, £20 for the organist and £10 for the choir. The choir was to be paid at the rate of six old pennies a week (three pence for morning service and threepence for afternoon or evening service, with an additional penny for practice if it took place). By the late nineteen-eighties the choir had become few in number and was augmented only for special occasions, when it would prepare a particular piece or two. Week by week there were a few good, strong voices (of whom Bea was one) who led the congregation. Needless to say the proceeds of the Slacke bequest did not reach the members of the choir. Bea made a po-faced intervention at a church meeting demanding to be informed what had happened to the choir's pay and bemoaning the trustees' neglect (no doubt forgetting that she was a trustee herself). Nowadays the choir has re-emerged.

There was another bequest. This was used to establish a bread charity. The object of this was to provide the needy, especially widows, with a loaf of bread every week. A sum was bequeathed by Samuel Wood to realise £2. 10s. per annum for the purpose. Willie remembers his brothers collecting loaves from the shop at New Smithy on their way to church for distribution to those chosen to be given the bread. One of the regular recipients was Hannah Furness, a local character who lived alone, except for the hens she kept in her house. She died in 1905 at the age of seventy-five. Willie remembers her for her 'ten petticoats which you could count.' She would appear at Chinley Chapel to collect her bread. When people came to visit her at her cottage near to Slacke Hall they were expected to bring something. A visit from Mr. Bagshawe, the descendant of William, was expected to yield a shilling, and when he said he had only a sovereign in his pocket, she gave him nineteen shillings change. The bread charity continued for many years and was given a new impetus by Willie's return, but eventually inflation had its inevitable effect and the spirit of the charity that it proffered was no longer appreciated. For a while an arrangement was made with a local shop that the recipients could have their bread at a cheaper rate, the charity meeting the difference. The fund was then reconstituted to enable the minister to give appropriate help at his own discretion.

One interesting statistic is the fact that there were more marriages conducted during the Simpson ministry at Chinley Chapel than in the entire two hundred and fifty years of the chapel's previous history. Some of this is accounted for by the fact that non-conformist churches for a long time, until 1837, were not licensed to conduct marriage ceremonies. On the other hand, for one hundred and twenty-eight years marriages had been permitted at Chinley Chapel. How then to account for the sudden and marked increase in numbers? There were couples in the district, especially the divorced, who failed to meet the conditions required of them by other churches, in particular the established church. Willie let it be known that they would be treated sympathetically at Chinley Chapel and so there came a steady flow of enquiries. His attitude was, as it always had been (and as described before), that if a person saw fit to come to him to ask to be married in church then there was enough of God in him. But that person needed to know, in the first place, that there was a minister in the district who held such a view. Willie made quite sure, without emblazoning the information anywhere, by a word here, a hint there, that as many as possible of those who needed to know were informed.

Nor did he apply any stringent conditions to the bringing of a child for baptism. As a result there were many families who were touched by the church and who found an accepting, non-judging Christianity. Willie well knew that for the majority of them, both children and wedding partners, this would be a fleeting touch. But he also knew that there would be those among them for whom the moment and the experience would be of some lasting meaning and he would never have been party to the loss of such an opportunity.

In the early years of the century an extension was built on to the Sunday School, to add two classrooms. The building was done by voluntary labour, by men who worked as builders for their living and then came to do the work on the chapel after their day's work and on Saturday afternoons. Not only that, they undertook to supply the stone for the building. This they did in turn at four shillings a load 'from Wicken quarry which was on the Glossop road towards Peep o'Day.' 'A very large contribution for all of them,' said Willie.

'It were a large slice out of their wages.' One of the men was another Joseph Waterhouse, a man not related to his namesake who was Willie's mentor. 'He had only a shilling a week spending money and yet he still took his turn.' Joseph was still living in the district when Willie returned to Chinley. Willie heard that he was seriously ill in hospital in Stockport and so decided to visit him.

'I went in and I said to the nurse' "How is Joseph Waterhouse?" And she said, "He's doing very nicely." I walked up to the bed and I said, "Joe, I've come to thank you for the work you did in building the Sunday School classrooms. When I think of your sacrifice I owe you a debt of gratitude along with all the other men. My word, I've never forgot and never shall." We talked a while and then I got up to go. He shook hands with me. His handshake was so faint I thought, "Joe, you'll be dead in the mornin'." I came out and I said to the sister, "How is Mr. Waterhouse actually?" She said, "Oh, he's fine." I said, "He'll be gone by mornin'." I met his daughter just as I was coming outside the door. She said, "Have you been to see father?" I said, "Yes, he'll be gone by mornin', dear. I'm goin' away on Saturday - to Morecambe. But," I said, "I shall come back to bury your father. Now you must telephone me in the morning to say whether he's here or not. Arrange the funeral and I'll come back here on the day." Eight o'clock next morning the telephone rang to say her father had died in the night and the funeral would be next Wednesday.'

'I got up at five o'clock and caught the bus out of Morecambe to Manchester. I wrote to the Cartledges who lived opposite the Manse to say I'll be coming from Morecambe to bury Joe Waterhouse. I shall be bringing some sandwiches from the hotel and I'll need a drink o' tea. And I spoke to Mr. Noblett in Edale and he met me at Manchester bus stop and brought me to Chinley Chapel. I conducted the funeral at twelve o'clock. My word, he was a marvellous man, this Joe Waterhouse. He was a good singer with a fine baritone voice. He won the prize at the Buxton Festival.' 'Immediately the service was over I said to the undertaker, "You're taking me back to Manchester, aren't you?" He said, "No, I've no instructions." I said, "I'm giving you the instructions. I said if you don't take me back to Manchester I'll see you're not paid." I said, "It's more than you're worth to leave me stranded 'ere. This family would be grieved beyond measure." He were goin' into Stockport or somewhere. He said, "You'll not catch the bus at two o'clock." I said, "I shall. The Lord'll never let me down." We got into the bus station and I stepped on to the first step and she pulls the trigger to start! We were on the move before I'm sat down.'

In 1971 the Congregational Union and the Presbyterian Church decided to merge to form the United Reformed Church. It would not be wrong to say that an important impulse behind this was financial. Many churches were operating on a very short shoestring and they felt that their only means of survival was to pool resources and to find joint strength. Within Congregational churches there was debate, democratic as the principles of the church's foundation would require. But the slant of the argument very much determined by the general state of the church building, the finances and the ability, actual and potential of the individual church to support its own minister. Some decided to join the new body. Fewer than half decided to remain outside it, the Congregational churches re-forming themselves ultimately into the Congregational Federation.

At Chinley there was a debate as elsewhere. An additional factor there was that the chapel was Independent first and Congregational next. The accident of its history at this juncture was that the minister was Willie Simpson who was, in his own words, 'a loyal congregationalist of an independent order' with the emphasis growing towards the end of the epithet. Willie gave his own account of the meeting which rejected the idea of joining the new body. There were arguments for and against, but the crucial moment, according to Willie, came when Miss Annie Nadin turned to Mrs. Winterbottom from Stoddart Farm during the course of the meeting and asked her what she thought. Mrs. Winterbottom, then of a good age and hard of hearing, needed explanation as to what was happening. When she understood she uttered with great force, 'Stop as we are!'

In many debates there is a catalytic moment and this was an unequivocal expression of the independence of Chinley Chapel if ever there was one. When the vote came to be taken there was a substantial majority in favour of 'stopping as we are.' Willie would never have entertained the thought of surrendering control of the church to a central governing body. 'All they're interested in is money,' he says. 'They need you to pay your way. And if you begin to struggle they'll close you down. What does an office in Liverpool know about what's going on at Chinley?' The irony of this comment will not be lost for many who know Willie. He did know, however, that his own efforts were on behalf of his own church and its congregation, maintaining its strength and looking for its continuing survival. Furthermore, it was effort from within itself and striving for self-sufficiency.

In 1973 Willie was given the minor distinction of appearing on BBC Radio's 'Down Your Way' during which he was interviewed, in best Sunday voice, by Brian Johnston as they sat together in Willie's 'blessed sanctuary'. This was an acknowledgment from the locality of Willie's place in its life. No account of Chapel-en-le-Frith would be complete without him.

For Chinley Chapel the early seventies saw the consolidation of the efforts made on Willie's arrival to get the church 'on a sound footing'. The new trust deed for the chapel, made necessary both because of a change in the law in respect of the Charity Commissioners and because of the trust fund established from the stipend Willie had foregone, was drawn up and finally signed in July, 1974 at Snitterton Hall, Matlock, the home of F. E. G. Bagshawe. The trustees' minutes record the steady growth of the fund and advice on long term investment.

Early in 1976 the minutes record that 'Rev. Simpson had intimated that the church should be thinking of a new minister. The news was received with regret, but understanding.' And then, 'Rev. Simpson would remain as Minister Emeritus.' The reason for this decision was that Ida's health and energy were failing, not drastically, but enough for her to feel that the duties of minister's wife were becoming beyond her. Thus Chinley Chapel began to look for a new minister. It was to be a fairly long process, Willie stating in July, 1976 that he 'would not relinquish the pastorate until a successor had been found'. The successor, Rev. J. L. Brooker, was, in fact, given the call in November and eventually took up the pastorate in April, 1977. Willie and Ida had completed nearly twelve years of 'retirement', doing the 'temporary' job they had come to do to help the church out of its difficulties.

When he returned to Chinley, Willie discovered some small tokens of the past. He unearthed a pocket watch which had been given to Rev. J. F. Moore, a previous minister of Chinley Chapel, inscribed 'Presented to J. F. M by a few friends of Chinley Chapel, 1899.' Willie gave this watch to his successor, as a memento of his office. He also recalled the fact that the rent of £1 per annum from a field at Shire Oaks, a farm near to Malcoff, was set aside for payment to the minister of Chinley Chapel. This was to be given to the minister on the first Sunday of the year by the trustees. He also re-established the church's connection with Brierley Green Congregational Church. He had, throughout his ministry at Chinley, conducted a service at Brierley Green once a month. He was very aware, probably more than anyone connected with Brierley Green, of the part played in the building of Brierley Green Church in 1826 by Rev. Ebenezer Glossop, who was minister of Chinley Chapel for fifty years. Willie's sense of history became stronger as he grew older.

Naturally this sense of history was to be put to a practical purpose. Brierley Green Church was no more than a quarter of a mile from the house in New Road, Buxworth, left by brother Harry for the Simpsons to retire to. And Brierley Green Church had never, in its 150-year history, had a minister of its own. Now they had the offer of a minister, one, moreover, who was prepared for the second time to accept no stipend, not even a token. The congregation of some twelve souls welcomed him.

There is a sense that in taking on another pastorate in the fifty-second year of his ministry, in continuing his working life after Chinley Chapel, that Willie had, so to speak, gone beyond his crowning days. He was in his seventy-ninth year when he left Chinley. Generally speaking, only politicians and gifted, timeless practitioners of the arts carry on so productively into advanced age - and the politicians can be known to outstay their welcome. At the age of seventy-eight, however, most members of the community would be expecting to retire, by reason of diminished energy or even the feeling of having earned a rest. There is no doubt that Ida felt this way. But Willie had found for himself yet another opportunity. He was to be able to close one very active chapter in his life and open a new one, needed by another church community to continue his lifelong mission.

And what of Chinley Chapel? It was back on its feet. It had regained its self-esteem and was flourishing. It was able to look from the end of one pastorate in the knowledge that it could begin a new one, with the means to support its own minister. The difficulty for this new minister was, as it had been at all the churches Willie had served in, to follow him. His single-mindedness, mild eccentricities, more noticeable in the anachronisms of old age, his sense of identity with Chinley and his abiding affection for the chapel, the affection offered by those who knew him, the gratitude for lifting the church out of its decline, the largeness of his personality, all this made it especially difficult at this time. Rev. Brooker had a very hard act to follow.

Rev. Brooker's predecessor was also to remain in the vicinity. This was the first time that Willie had remained physically close to a pastorate he was relinquishing. It must have been difficult for him to become an onlooker, especially as it was the church that was closest to his heart throughout a long life. His concern with the affairs of the church was to continue for many years after his departure. As his hand was withdrawn from the helm and his influence diminished and the trustees began to make recommendations to the church meeting, particularly about the spending of money on capital projects, money which Willie thought should have been left to secure the pastorate, he was to become increasingly uncomfortable, if not frustrated and annoyed at the 'profligacy' he perceived.

Being at a greater distance, where he would not have had regular contact with people from the church might have helped to mitigate these feelings, but that was not likely to have been significant given that it was the welfare of Chinley Chapel which was occupying his mind. Nevertheless the passage of time, the needs of Ida and his own instincts told him that the moment to move on, even from Chinley Chapel, had arrived. He was going to pastures, not quite new to him, in that Brierley Green was the church where he had preached his first sermon at the age of eighteen, but they gave him a fresh challenge as the first minister of its own that Brierley Green Congregational Church had had in the one hundred and fifty years of its existence.

10

Brierley Green

The church at Brierley Green was originally known as Bugsworth Independent Chapel. 'Bugsworth' has now become 'Buxworth'', not by any natural dynamic of the language, but by a conscious decision before the nineteen-twenties in an attempt to make the name less 'undignified'. Willie remembers the vicar and the schoolmaster being the prime movers in the change of name. Various options were considered - Red Wharf Dale and Lime Dale, for example, but the name finally chosen did at least have the merit of minimal administrative change. Willie ponders on how he used to pronounce 'Bugsworth' as a boy. The stress seemed to have been on the first vowel, a 'u' uttered uncompromisingly with lips thrust forward, vintage Derbyshire - and vintage Simpson. The hardness of the 'g' could be said to have reflected the rigours of existence of the time. Survival was, for many people, the first priority. You flourished rarely. The change to 'Buxworth' softened the consonant, flattened the vowel and gave greater stress to the second syllable, producing an altogether more effete sound, the kind of sound which Willie would affect in the pulpit or in the company of a person whom he believed to be higher class. It is interesting that this change of name of the neighbouring village of his youth reflects something of his own development. However, the cricket ground on Western Lane still resounds to 'Come on, Buggie!'

To quote the little history of the chapel, (written in 1906 to begin an appeal for funds when it was decided to extend the building)

'. . . in the year 1827 the cause was established. The building when erected was not intended for a Congregational chapel. It was built (in the year 1826) entirely by public subscriptions, the labour of carting stones, &c, being done voluntarily by the farmers and team owners of the village. There is in the front wall a stone tablet bearing the following inscription: "This School was erected by public subscription, 1826, pro bono publico." The place was first opened as a Day and Sunday School for the whole of Bugsworth and in those days writing and arithmetic were taught in the Sunday School. . . . . . The first Trust Deed of the place was executed in March 1828. . . . . The Deeds specified that the Day School Teachers should reside upon the premises, there being an upper as well as a lower room. . . . . Soon after the opening of the Day School, the Rev. Ebenezer Glossop, who was the Congregational Minister at Chinley Chapel for fifty years and upwards, was invited to hold Divine Services in the School and continued his labours for about thirty years. At the time he took charge there was a debt of £70 on the building. Mr. Glossop very generously and gratuitously gave his services until the debt was cleared off.'

Willie said, 'Rev. Glossop got farmers to make a public subscription. It would be the Bagshawes, the Slacks and the Bennetts who found most of the money.

Thereafter the connection with Chinley Chapel was maintained more and more tenuously. Two ministers of Chinley Chapel at the turn of the century, Rev. Moore and Rev. Shuttleworth, suffered from ill-health and advanced age, respectively, and were unable to make the journey to Bugsworth. Then, 'After the death of Sam Heath in 1922,' Willie recalls, 'Brierley Green began to die. The church turned more towards Whaley Bridge. But Willie's intimate knowledge of the history of both churches and his instinct for the continuance of tradition revived the tie when he came to Chinley Chapel in 1965.

Samuel Heath, first to give Willie the opportunity to preach in May, 1916, was the mentor of Brierley Green Church for many years. He served the church from 1875 until his death in 1922. As president of the Manchester, Salford and District Lay Preachers Society he developed a special interest in Brierley Green, which sustained the church against all odds. His service is commemorated on a marble plaque in the church. "A labourer in his Master's vineyard for 85 years," forty seven of them closely connected with Brierley

Green. Willie remembers him with reverence and gratitude. 'He were a minister in every possible sense. He enjoyed great respect. What he said were like a command. He devoted a lot of attention to me, finding me preaching appointments. He was a widower. He spent half the week at Bugsworth, staying at Mrs. Cotterill's. He was a forceful personality and a delightful preacher. I remember him preaching at Chinley Chapel while I was blowing the organ. He used wonderful illustrations in his sermons. I always thought I must find good illustrations for my own sermons, just like Samuel Heath.'

He was man after Willie's own heart, described in an obituary leaflet as one who 'zealously upheld the right of every Church in the Congregational Order to maintain its individuality. The name independent was a reality to him, and he held tenaciously to this conviction. . . . . . His character was a happy blend of the emotional and the practical. . . . . . . He was always suspicious of, and held aloof from large organisations; he was very doubtful of the reputed efficiency of elaborate church machinery. "The daily round and the common task" appealed more to his simple tastes. In his judgment of men he was generally reliable. In doubtful cases where his opinion was solicited his remark would be, "If you cannot do a man any good, do him no harm." It is easy to see how such a man became an important model for the young Willie Simpson. The man described could well be Willie himself. Willie felt that after Sam Heath died the church 'ran down'. It is not good for any institution that it should become too reliant on an individual.

Willie's first memory of the Independent Chapel at Bugsworth was in 1905 when he was aged seven. He was taken to an evening service in the winter by Norman Kirk. Ninety years later he could point to the place where he sat. His next visit was as a preacher when he was almost eighteen. Thereafter he appeared regularly in the pulpit ('They would come to me when they were stuck fast.') until he went to college. While at college he continued to pay visits to the chapel but on a much less regular basis. He preached at the memorial service to Samuel Heath ('It was on the 9th July 1922'). After leaving college he came to Brierley Green once while he was at Mexborough. He hardly visited the church at all in the interim, until his return to Chinley. 'But I always knew everythin' that were goin' off from when I used to visit Mother. Folks at Chinley always went to special events at Brierley Green. That kept us in touch.'

One event especially in the history of Brierley Green Congregational Church illustrates a spirit of independence reminiscent of Chinley Chapel. In drawing up the original Trust Deed it had been stipulated that there should be a minimum of three Trustees. In 1890, through either deaths, defections or overlooking the implications, the number of Trustees diminished to two.

Consequently the Charity Commissioners were obliged to put the School up for auction. Those connected with chapel assumed that they would be entitiled to bid for their own building and resume ownership for a nominal sum. Unfortunately, a local man, an adjoining landowner, had designs on the place and was bidding against them, so that in the end they had to pay £205, an enormous sum. The secretary, Thomas Hadfield, was bidding on behalf of the church. As the bidding progressed he had to be shored up by the others around him. As the history of the church relates, 'Some spirited bidding took place, our opponent offering £200; this caused the spirits of the teachers and friends to droop; others, however, were not to be daunted, and they stimulated and urged Mr. Hadfield to bid on. 'The money they paid had already been raised with the intention of enlarging the building. It must have been very galling to have had to pay such a sum merely to retain ownership of their place of worship. Sixteen or seventeen years later the money was raised again and the building considerably extended. It was doubled in size and transformed very visibly from Bugsworth Independent Chapel into Brierley Green Congregational Church.

There remains a minute book of the Trustees meetings, beginning on 2nd February, 1891, a small, pocket-sized memorandum book (from 'S. Proctor, Printer, Stationer and Bookseller, Dealer in Fancy Goods, Openshaw, Manchester - One Penny'). The opening page lists twenty Trustees. They did not intend to be caught again. The list of occupations of the Trustees is indicative of the character of the district at the time, and a pointer to the world of Willie's childhood. Brierley Green is a mile from Whitehough and Chinley. There are lime burners, a lime piker, a collier, a boat man, a signalman, a cotton weaver, a paper maker, an agent and merchant, a coal merchant, a minister (of New Mills Congregational Church) and 'a gentleman'. At the time an important industry in Bugsworth was the lime-kilns. The pair of semi-detached houses built by Harry Simpson on New Road where Willie came to live was built on the site of lime-kilns. The stone for the kilns was brought down a tramway from Dove Holes and Peakdale, passing through Chapel Milton and Whitehough on its journey. The coal for lime burning was mined by Dolly Lane near to Laneside Farm. Boats coming into the canal basin at Bugsworth, reached by an arm of the Peak Forest Canal, took away the finished product, lime. The area was much more industrial in those days than it is now.

Now, the dominant feature of the valley is the by-pass. This has separated the two halves of Buxworth village. The half where Willie lives has the Anglican church and the post office, the school and the Memorial Club. Below, near to the canal basin, as the name would suggest, is the Navigation

Inn. Then there is a stretch of a quarter of a mile or so before the road crosses the by-pass on a bridge. There is also a foot bridge. Western Lane, the other half of Buxworth, contours the other side of the valley, the southern side. A terrace of stone cottages overlooks a football pitch and a diminutive cricket ground. Beyond these, on the northern side, is Brierley Green below the dominant features of Chinley Churn and Cracken Edge.

The Manchester to Sheffield railway line bridges the road through Brierley Green twice within a couple of hundred yards, which separates it from Buxworth. A steep climb enters the hamlet under the first railway bridge, past some 'modern' semi-detached, thence to a row of variegated stone cottages, past Dolly Lane for a further hundred or so yards to the Congregational Church, just by the other railway bridge. If you are motoring in either direction it is easy to be past the church without being aware that it is there because the bends in the road and the bridge need the driver's attention.

The church is not an attractive building. Originally it was a stone rectangle with simple rectangular windows, stark, functional, but with an appeal founded in its proportion and simplicity. All the basic lines were vertical and horizontal. When the building was extended, this involved putting another 'building' across one end, creating a 'T' shape which at least doubled its capacity. The new part was given windows with arches; there are pediments, buttresses and other embellishments. An entrance porch, with an arched doorway and surmounting pediment has been put into the angle between the new and the old buildings. It does not feel like a successful marriage, but it is a clear expression of the determination of the members that this was a building set aside for worship. It was not to be allowed to become merely the dwelling it almost became in 1890.

The interior is 'sideways on' like Chinley Chapel. The pews, the lectern and the woodwork are all ornate in the Victorian/Edwardian way with no lightness of touch. There is little of the simplicity to be found in Chinley Chapel. The preacher presides from a central position, the strong leadership of congregationalism. There are marble memorials to Samuel Heath and Hannah Cotterill. The roof space has carved trusses and black metal ties, a void with none of the intimacy and warmth of Chinley Chapel.

This was another changing point in Willie's life. When he returned to Chinley Chapel, certainly when the 'temporary' nature of the pastorate began to be dispelled, he may well have believed that he would end his days of active ministry there. But, having acknowledged that his time there was at an end, he found that he still had working energy. There would be no looking backwards, without any doubt. He had something new to get hold of, another set of souls to minister to and another building with 'an open mouth'. Both were the kind of challenge he relished.

This was one of the least attractive of his churches, architecturally, but for Willie the focus was, as always, the maintenance and improvement of the fabric, not aesthetics. He was sensitive to the atmosphere of his churches; winter evenings in Chinley Chapel showed how much he could be touched, but in the end, the practical work of sustaining the place for worship was his first preoccupation.

'When I was at Mexborough I used to wish for a few old people among the congregation,' he says. 'What do you think I wish for at Brierley Green?' It is certainly true, in Willie's nineties, that he has the regular duty of conducting the funerals of church members. And yet the number attending services somehow keeps to a steady twelve. Brierley Green's Special Occasions are two a year - the Anniversary in April and the Old-Fashioned Sing in September. These are the occasions when the church is full of people. Support is drummed up in the long-practised way. For several weeks beforehand people are reminded of the occasion, by personal call, by telephone or by letter. The letter is accompanied by a leaflet announcing the service and listing donors and their financial contributions in the previous year. They are hinted at, invited, asked, maybe exhorted (but never told) to come to the service. Brierley Green church has its own page in the Chinley Chapel magazine and the Minister writes that 'the Anniversary (or the Old-Fashioned Sing) is upon us. All are welcome to this great occasion.' There are musical guests, singers such as Jessie Gregory, John Biddulph and Peter Morris, choirs such as the Whaley Bridge Ladies and the Chapel-en-le-Frith Male Voice Choir. They come to sing simply because it is Willie who has asked them to.

One year the Male Voice Choir was not available for the Anniversary as usual on the appointed date. This entailed a reorganisation which set in train a series of 'things going wrong'. 'Everything's gone wrong for the Anniversary, everything,' said Willie. 'But I'm not goin' to let it break me. I think I've made a hundred visits, written fifty letters and made thirty telephone calls. It's been a nightmare. But it'll go through. If it's going to be a success you've got to work at it and be determined.' Of course it did 'go through', and very successfully. It is significant that there was a preponderance of visits over letters and telephone calls. '£150 has come through subscriptions. It hasn't come by sittin' back.'

In the face of the deafness of his old age it is difficult to know how much Willie can hear of the lovely music being performed for him. He sits on the lofty dais at the front of the church looking hard, as if straining to see, head turning slowly from one side of the congregation to the other, mouth half open almost in a grimace. The sheer volume of sound from the choirs, especially the male choir, must surely penetrate, but whether he hears or not, the occasion, the detailed, accurate memory of words and music, especially of Handel oratorio in its great strength and uplift, carries him aloft. And, as Joy Needham remarked, 'The latest Special Occasion was always the best he remembered. And at the age of ninety what more can you ask? There is no looking back to past glories when you can find such joy in the present. '

The Old-Fashioned Sing has a long history. In 1989, Robert Hadfield, the church secretary for many years, produced a short account of the tradition. It arose in 1907 when efforts were continuing to raise funds to extend the church building. 'It was suggested that a string orchestra be formed to recapture the days of old when there was neither organ nor piano and the singing of hymns was accompanied by string or wind instrument . . . . . . In preparation for the first Old-Fashioned Sing music books of hymn tunes were hand written by the Cotterill family [and] duplicated for the use of the orchestra and sold to the public for 3d a copy.' Some of these astounding examples of painstaking, elegant draughtsmanship still exist, too precious almost to use. If nothing else, they are a symbolic survival of the church's will to survive, the living, thriving determination which is so much Willie Simpson.

The Brierley Green congregation was delighted at the prospect of acquiring its own minister, but perhaps because it was a venerable group it proved itself to be less malleable for Willie than his previous flocks. There were some irritations. 'There is one thing about a church that has never had a minister,' he remarked. 'Lay men that have got hold of a key, they'll never let it go. One man had the safe key on a nail in his bedroom. Three or four people had a key to the church door. If they'd had any sense at all they'd have said, "Mr. Simpson should have a key." I got the safe key when the man became too ill. I was told I should have insisted. But that's all right. You're dealing with people at eighty and odd that's held these keys for fifty years or something of that kind. So, of course, I bided my time. And after all's done and said I never hurt them. I might have done a lot of damage. If I'd have been a younger man I might have been a bit more cheeky, but, you see, as you've grown older you've grown with people and you think to yourself, "What's the use of offending them?" I'm an 'owd 'ead. I know what they'd say. "I've had my key all these many years and now they've taken it from me." They'd never been used to a minister.'

For Ida there was similar need to adjust to changing circumstances. It was entirely new for the congregation at Brierley Green to have its own minister. They had, therefore, never had to consider the position of the minister's wife. There were many fewer people to attend to, which must have been of some comfort to Ida, still no doubt wondering when retirement would actually begin. Nevertheless, some adjustment was still needed on her part to the long-established practices and attitudes of their new pastorate. Her perceptiveness and tact became even more important. Both she and Willie felt that it was they, and not the people of the church, who should adapt. They had an old congregation. They knew how change could affect the old.

On August 2nd 1982, when Ida woke up she found herself unable to get out of bed. She had had a stroke. She had lost the use of her right arm and her right leg but still had the power of speech. By the end of the day she was in the cottage hospital in Buxton. Willie said, 'After that I was never given any indication that she would be fit enough to come home.' At that time his age was eighty-four, and notwithstanding his continuing health and vitality, it would have been beyond him to have managed Ida at home. As the months passed by she did say that she would have liked to have come home, but she acknowledged that the care that she would have needed was more than Willie could cope with. So she resigned herself to a long stay in hospital and may well have understood that she would never go home. Then, as Christmas approached, she began to decline further. Willie was visiting the hospital afternoon and evening every day except Sunday when he missed the afternoon visit because of afternoon service at Brierley Green. He was very aware of how his beloved 'Auntie' was failing. His helpmate of forty-eight years of marriage and several years before that, finally died on 29th January 1983. She was seventy-nine years old.

The sister on the hospital ward asked on the evening after Ida's death whether Willie had anyone to stay with him. Willie said there was no-one. She was concerned and pressed the point. He replied that he would have the company of 'an unseen comrade'. She understood.

Ida and Willie, at the time of their engagement, had publicly consecrated their lives together to the service of God. When they married each had taken the other 'with God's help'. That Willie should feel the presence of his 'unseen comrade' at this time of loss is no surprise. Ida and Willie had fulfilled their pledge for nearly fifty years, complementary natures, the sum of the parts greater than the individual parts together in their work. 'If I were shinin' she 'eld back. If she were shinin' I 'eld back. If she spoke anywhere, at a ladies' meeting or such, she wasn't happy unless I were in the back pew. And she knew about folk. I could always trust her judgment, even if I couldn't understand why she had doubts at the time. 'Did you have any differences of opinion?' 'Oh, yes, but it didn't make any difference. We were allowed to think what we wanted, but there was no ill feeling.'

The role of minister's wife is difficult. The first difficulty is that the husband's job is explicitly a vocation. The demands on the husband are many and varied. The job is open-ended, the flock open-mouthed. There is a need for clear boundaries so that the undertaking can be manageable. The chances are that the man will not be able draw his own boundaries, so that the wife will feel it incumbent that she draws them for him. This blurs their mutual boundaries and it can cast her as protector and barrier between minister and flock. On the other hand she can leave him to make his own judgments and maintain his own role, which lays her open to the accusation of remoteness and a lack of concern. Too much concern and she is interfering; undue concern with some elements of the church and she is showing favour. The path is a delicate one to tread.

Ida trod this path unerringly. Willie's admiration for her ability to tread this role was enormous. He loved her for herself, her quiet, dignified demeanour, her gentle humour, her sensitivity and her awareness. He held her in reverence for her ability and her judgment. For him she was the ideal wife for a minister, a support to him in his vocation, and also equally important, capable of her own ministry among the people, in her own way, at the same time. She was described as 'constantly at his shoulder, a half-pace behind, but forever there in her own right', an attentive ear to be given, time always to spare. Nobody has demurred from this view. Whereas people recalled Willie with a mixture of affection, admiration and amusement at his idiosyncrasies of manner, of appearance and of approach to duty, and of some irritation at his occasional obduracy, when they spoke of Ida, tones would soften and there is a smile of love and respect, expressions resonant of her own manner. People who went to her felt valued. Thus, she was recognised for herself, but she was also demonstrably the minister's wife. Having become the minister's wife gave her special talents the opportunity to flourish. Without each other Ida and Willie would have been diminished.

Ida was buried at Chinley Chapel. Many people came from Mexborough, from Enderby and especially from Blakenall and Ryecroft to pay their respects. Her grave is the first one you see as you enter the church yard from the car park by the Joe Ford Gate. Now, the name, Simpson, is the first one you see as you pass through the gate. Ida has played a part in asserting the name once more in the annals of the chapel - in her own characteristically unobtrusive and unexpected way.

Willie took this loss as he took the other losses in his life - we are all mortal, something which is perhaps easier to accept as we get older. Earlier losses, such as the return of Branwen to her family, both he and Ida felt very acutely. In retrospect that loss was inevitable, but they had persuaded themselves that it was not going to happen. When it did the pain was very great. When Ida died the pain of loss and the emptiness of home were hard for

Willie but bearable. He felt what many who have been widowed must feel, surrounded as they are by all the accumulations of a shared life, the furniture, the draperies, the crockery and all the unsuspected minutiae. He felt the comfort of these reminders and he felt the void that they signified. Years later he was moved to carry out one of Ida's wishes; to sell some of their things and, especially, some of hers, to raise money 'for the missionary society'. Going through the drawers, taking out pillow cases and table cloths, crocheted to a delicate tracery by Auntie, finding leather gloves and woollen cardigans that she had worn, brought back her lost presence. He came down stairs with an armful of goods, muttering, 'Oh dear, oh dear. ' It was a hard thing he had set himself to do. But the sale on a Friday evening was a happy occasion. It did not raise much money but Ida would have liked the happy atmosphere, the gathering in her name - though scarcely any present knew of this fact.

In July, 1985 Willie completed sixty years of continuous, active ministry. This remarkable fact came to the notice of Mark Greteson, a minister who held office in the Central School of Religion, founded in 1896 in Surrey, England and in Indiana, U. S. A. The truly remarkable aspect of Willie's service was that it was in the full ministry. Mark Greteson knew of no other minister who had done service in such a way for sixty years. There may well have been ministers who had served for forty, or even fifty years and then, having retired, returned to take occasional Sunday services as a supply. As Willie said, 'They would have gone away at the end of the service with no responsibility, not to be in charge of a church.' Mark Greteson believed Willie's service deserved recognition. The Central School of Religion therefore decided to confer on Willie an Honorary Doctorate of Divinity. Initially he was reluctant to accept. He felt he was not worthy, no doubt remembering his estimation of Rev. Hedgman in Nottingham, whose doctorate, as Willie always said, was conferred 'by examination'. But friends prevailed on him to accept and he was persuaded. The honour was conferred with due ceremony, in the presence of fellow ministers and representatives of the Congregational churches in the High Peak on 20th July,1985. So the boy who began packing parcels of towelling seventy years before in Hadfield's works was now 'Reverend Doctor', entitled to bring into the Sunday service a splash of bright red and yellow in the academic hood he now wore over his gown. - a right Willie was very happy to exercise.

Chinley Chapel also played its part in marking this day. A new door was needed at the east end of the chapel. The replacement, a substantial and solid portal of oak, was installed and a commemorative plaque put in the chapel. It has become 'The Simpson Door'. It was a great joy to Willie that he should become the means by which people gain access to his 'beloved sanctuary'.

This also recalled for him the boyhood memory of those who used the door for services, 'the minister, the Bagshawes, the Slacks, the Bennetts, the organist and the organ blower'. It is likely that the honour given to him by the chapel was of much greater significance to him than the doctorate.

Willie's ministry at Brierley Green was to continue for more years after Ida's death than during her lifetime. It is now approaching being his longest ministry, an astounding fact when one recalls his 'retirement' at least twenty-seven years before to Chinley Chapel. It has been an even longer ministry than both Mexborough and Enderby. The significant contrast, though, has been in the amount achieved. His day still follows the long-established routine; rise early, read, prepare the next sermon in the morning; visits in the afternoon, now no more than three. 'Where do you go for these visits?' 'Oh, around Brierley Green and Buxworth,' which involved not a little walking, 'in Chapel and Whaley Bridge, and I go to the nursing homes in Buxton.' He gets about to the more distant places by his well-tried, time-honoured methods - but now relying on the availability of friends' cars (their use as ever obliquely requested) more than on chance lifts. But in the last resort he would simply step out of the front door of his house and wave down the first passing car 'the Lord not letting him down'.

In the zeal of his youth he had moved mountains at Mexborough. At Brierley Green it felt as though he were trying to move a mountain. Of all his churches it is the one least disposed to respond to his artfulness. It was set in its ways. It would not be changed. Is this because it was the church closest to his own beginnings, the church whose rustic obduracy, which accounts so much for its survival for so long, is the very strand of Willie's being which had enabled him to prevail. Or is it because there has been no 'Auntie' for so much of the ministry to observe shrewdly, to temper Willie and divert him from fruitless paths? Or is it that, in spite of being hale and vital well into his nineties, even a Willie Simpson must slow down? The answer may well be in all three factors. Nevertheless the members of his congregation value his leadership and wonder at his energy and his optimism as he continues to celebrate successive anniversaries of his ordination - currently almost seventy years.

At the time of writing the Brierley Green 'story' continues. The church is the source of greater anxiety to him than any other, he does not deny. He worries about its future. 'What will happen when I'm gone?' is a frequent question. Some people are certain that the church would not have continued had he not been there. Given the history of this place of worship there is room for doubt of this assertion, with due acknowledgment to modern times. Nevertheless Willie has done his best to assure Brierley Green's life, hinting here and manipulating there. But he has never got the solid reassurance that he wants. In the end, of course, what will happen is beyond his control, and he is the first to acknowledge it. The matter is in God's hands and Willie will do what the Christian does in the face of the intractable. He will let go and hand it over. The future is secure.

11

The Simpson Sermon

The Simpson Sermon begins with a prayer for the illumination of the Word. It then continues with the words, 'My subject is.....' There is invariably a text. If there were no text 'it would not be a sermon.' It would be 'an address'. The text is as likely to be from the Old Testament as the New. 'I think they forget nowadays what a wealth of wisdom is to be found in the Old Testament.' The structure is unchanging. After the text and the appropriate reference, the opening statement deals with its meaning, its import. Then follows a series of illustrations: personal, historical, geographical, from literature, art, music, and so on. As far as possible the illustrations derive directly from the experience of William Simpson. Sometimes there are illustrations he has found inspiring from others' lives, others' sermons - fine words, a place, an artefact, a landscape. In order to be touched by this inspiration Willie has needed to experience it at first hand. This has given his travels abroad a pilgrim's focus. To have gone abroad simply to 'take a holiday' would have been impractical, even frivolous. Nor would it have been true value for money. The purpose was to make the sermon rich in illustration, not simply in quantity, but in its thrust, its relevance and authenticity. Thus the sermon would be a path to joy and uplift. Being Christian is a happy business.

Willie has vivid boyhood recollections of the boredom of the dry, theological discourses of Rev. Shuttleworth in Chinley Chapel, and of Arthur's ability to recall them almost verbatim. The content was less memorable to Willie, who believed the sermon's subject and treatment should be, above all, accessible to the congregation and manageable in length. Joe Waterhouse was a good model and twenty to twenty-five minutes was enough. With good illustration the homily lived. Another model was T. De Witt Talmage, a nineteenth-century American Baptist from New York. It was Talmage's example that made Willie strive to provide all illustration from direct experience. In the introduction to his second volume of sermons Talmage says, 'The religion of Christ is never in all the Bible represented in darkness. It is a lantern. It is daybreak. It is a noontide glory. It is an irradiation. More than that, our religion is warmth.' The words and the style are essential Simpson.

I first heard a Simpson sermon as he approached his ninetieth year. His presence in Chinley Chapel pulpit was a surprise. I had expected the church's own minister, Rev. Bill Bentham. Willie's arrival was arresting. He had the particular radiance which came when he returned to the chapel. The shuffling, scurrying gait of his old age brought him in at a sixty-year-old's pace. Deafness accentuated reliance on eyesight - sharp, discrimating despite spectacles. From the pulpit he peered in all directions with half-straining eyes and without a grain of self-consciousness, the half-grimace of intense interest and concern, dissolving into a smile of recognition for familiar faces. Then he rose, the body straightened, the shoulders braced, the head uplifted, the chin, the strong, determined Simpson chin, jutted. 'Let us worship God.'

The voice is the pulpit voice. The tones are ringing, the vowels consciously flattened, the residue of the need to be 'acceptable'. Still, though, there is the Derbyshire voice, sometimes consciously summoned, other times asserting itself unbidden, not to be ignored. Always Derbyshire makes its point by contrast, usually in digression from the main theme. Little stories are shared as though they are confidences, a conspiracy we are invited to join. There is a suspicion of self-mockery. For a moment Willie comes down from the pulpit and shares a few secrets. We smile with him, even at him, indulgently. Then Rev. Dr. William Simpson re-ascends and resumes the discourse. We have had lightness. Now for renewed gravitas.

The effect, at the first time of hearing, was surprising. This living anachronism provoked curiosity. What was said and the way it was said were very much of his era - even earlier than his era. Yet the message was timeless. The prayers were plainly well practised and well worn, redolent of the King James Bible. The language carried Willie along, giving him time to think what he would say next, but the prayers spoke for everyone. There was a flood of feeling in the church, a one-ness.

Willie always has been an anachronism. People remarked on the middle-aged maturity of his outlook when he was younger than twenty. But he was 'without time' in a truly spiritual sense, with the charm of mild eccentricity, an out-dated unselfconsciousness, an unswerving sense of unfashionable purpose - all expressions of Divine benevolence and humour. Here was an essentially good man chosen to touch those whose lives he passed through. We are made in the image of God. We are imperfect in that image. But we have it in us to express the God in us. Willie Simpson reveals the God in himself and seeks to discover the God in those he touches. 'And those who seek God,' he said, 'need only look before them and see Him in mankind. It is God within who displays God without.' One of Willie's sermons quotes Charles Reade: 'Not a day passes but men and women of no note do great deeds, speak great works, suffer noble sorrows.'

The delivery of the sermon had been refined, honed over the years. In conversation Willie occasionally repeats a word or a phrase for emphasis, slowing the pace, savouring the point, giving it more weight. He does the same in the pulpit but in a broader measure. This gives the sermon a measured pace. A twenty-five minute sermon, written verbatim, occupies only two sides of A4. There is time to digest and consider. The thrust is simple but the lasting impression of the message is of strength - in delivery and in its import. A sermon on "Sincerity' (the text: 'Now fear the Lord and serve Him in sincerity and truth.' Joshua 24, v.14) asserted that 'There is a contagion in the real and the genuine and the truth.' 'Contagion' is not a common word these days, especially in such a context. Illustrations and particular points are often made in threes, these with frequent alliteration. 'Despair' is tied with 'despondency' and 'desperation'. The sermon will often end with a ringing exhortation, often, as in the case of this one, a clear statment of faith:

'Let us not forget that we are all Christ's children, his agents and his workmanship. Let us so live that others may want to possess the same living spirit that Joshua possessed. Let us so live that people may not see us but Christ who dwelleth in us. May we so live, true agents of Jesus Christ that we may warm the earth where'er we tread.

'Walk in the Lord that we may know
The fellowship of love,
That we may find God's Joy and Peace
In Sincerity Divine.'

The amalgam is nineteenth century oratory made accessible, but for many a young twentieth century ear, heard with an amused curiosity. On the other hand, a sixth form teacher of politics and economics said that she wished her students, most of them aspiring to university, could construct their essays as succinctly as Willie did his sermons.

A mid-morning visit to Willie in his nineties will often find him sitting at the dining table by the window which overlooks his back garden. Before him there will be a sheet of paper, an old Boots' Jotting Diary, the pages covered with his fine, clear, steady, well-shaped handwriting, not a square inch uncovered - reminiscent of Joe Waterhouse's economy of paper. The matter before him is anything up to seventy years old, sermons composed on a multiplicity of themes, all speaking of the One Great Theme. "Do you know, I've just got out my sermon on .... and I can't really improve it.' He rises at six-thirty and is soon at work on the sermons for next Sunday, spending most of the time in the way he has spent his mornings for seventy years. Now there is rarely a new sermon. The old ones are dusted off and polished. I mused that he must have given over seven thousand sermons in his lifetime.

He received this fact blankly. What you have to say next Sunday is all that matters.

'I should not want to live if I hadn't got a sermon to prepare, you know.' The theatre of the pulpit, the performance, are enticing, but God's work in His presence in His house is vital. On the other hand there is no slavish devotion to the sermon. If there are other things to be done, especially people to be seen, the old and the sick to be visited, they take precedence.

To find the measure of Willie Simpson's life, visit the churches and the places where he has been a minister. The work that he has done and his place in the hearts and minds of the people tell the story. Read his sermons to discover his values. The figures from history who are his examples come largely from the nineteenth century: David Livingstone, Florence Nightingale, the Earl of Shaftesbury and others, all of them enlightened, liberal thinkers in their day, respecters of mankind, advocates of the dignity of man, nowadays seen often to personify the white man and the superior Victorian Briton. We could accuse such people now of being racially and socially patronising but in their time they were humanity's caretakers. They saw the humanity in all mankind and did what they could to foster it which is what placed them so high in Willie's esteem.

Willie's great political heroes are David Lloyd George and Winston Churchill. He has never expressed an overt political allegiance. It is not for a minister to dabble in politics, nor to get himself involved in any political controversy. Possibly he felt too much gratitude in his youth to his 'superiors' to question any social injustice he might have perceived. You simply 'got on with it' and made the best of things as his mother had done. Nevertheless his choice of political hero gives some insight into his political bent. 'I suppose if I could call myself anything I would be a Liberal,' he said. The rural community of his formative years was conservative, if not Tory, suspicious of radicalism it saw as being fomented by trade unions. Men were supposed to know their place.

The qualities of Lloyd George and Churchill which Willie admired most were their charismatic leadership, their great strength and determination in the face of adversity, and their oratorical skills. Both men had a more dubious side, skills of manipulation and of wheeling and dealing. Either Willie did not see or chose to ignore these sides of their character. Maybe there was an instinctive admiration for the manipulative skills. Certainly his belief in strong leadership has been evident in all his pastoral work. He has led by example, and his churches have been pleased to follow, by and large. Some have been uncomfortable with his dogmatism and occasional inflexibility. Others have seen these flaws more than tempered by his simple, open-armed Christianity.

'Nothing is worthwhile if it is achieved easily. The best things in life come from toil, hard work and sacrifice.' This is a common Simpson theme. Satisfaction comes to Willie when sitting by the evening fireside with a good day's work well done. He always works hard and he always enjoys his work. He likes to motivate and enable others to work. The most telling example of this was at Blakenall where the sum of the Simpson and Smith parts was so much greater than the two parts. This also enabled and encouraged others to make their own contributions, and gave that church the vibrancy which characterised it in Willie's day. The nice irony was that there seemed to be an ease in the commitment which suggested that things were easily achieved, belying the corporate effort.

Willie saw another irony in this quotation from Coleridge, made in a sermon on "Hard Work".

'Genius alone cannot make you great.
There must be industry to second skill.
Faith, tireless perseverance, strength of will
Ere triumph and success upon you wait.
Would'st though obtain fame's ragged frowning steep
It must be thine to toil while others sleep.'

The irony is that these lines were from the hand of a man whose life and talents were laid to waste by opium addiction. The poignancy is surely in Coleridge's awareness of this need for self-discipline through the window of the wreck of his own life. Strangely, the lines also capture the uncomplicated essence of Willie Simpson, for whom distractions such as those which dogged Coleridge seemed never to have been remotely near. Yet to read the sermon in which these lines occur there is intrinsic compassion throughout for the poet. 'There but for the grace of God...'

Old age discards the superfluous. The simplicity of Willie's life's mission is very clear in his old age. He is grateful to God for his gift of ministry. He is grateful for the many years of opportunity to exercise it. There have been obstacles and setbacks at times in his life, but almost always these have been met with relish. 'A setback to many has often proved to be a stepping stone,' he has told his congregations more than once. 'The irksome things are part of the making of life.' We can sometimes see before us 'stern reality, the iron gate,' but it is 'the angels of everyday life, folk just like you' who open the iron gate. And 'the iron gate is not opened by force but by love'. We should be 'lubricating the gates of life with brotherly love and kindness.' We do not deliberately seek 'the stern realities'. Rather we acknowledge that they will from time to time confront us, unavoidably, but it is only through love and kindness that we can deal with them.

'At the root of the distraction of life is the lack of love and affection when young,' said Willie in another sermon. This is a truism we so regularly forget. Freud, Erikson, Bowlby, and others eminent in psychology, all speak of the effects of sound and unsound beginnings. Identity, self, a sense of self, the boundaries around self, the boundaries between self and other are fostered by a loving beginning. The child is valued, but there are also demands and expectations. The child is loved enough to be helped to his feet and supported if he totters, but he is loved enough also to be expected to walk and to develop his own equilibrium, to learn the bounds beyond which there is danger of hurt to self or other, and loved enough to suffer restraint if these bounds are impinged. This is the kind of love and affection which Wille received as a child and which he advocates. In this way, as he would say, 'We are writing a new gospel every day.'

Willie has had a clear sense of purpose to his life from a very tender age. Life has always been ordered. It is important to him that he should know where he stands. The routine of his daily life, the way he carries out all his tasks reflects this. He is law-abiding, an advocate of the well-ordered society (but this would never preclude the imaginative bending of rules to make things better for the needy). 'God's power behind our life gives a place, a seat, a setting in the scheme of life. Life is a cherished possession. Life is wonderful if lived with a purpose.' This sense of order and focus have given him a sense of security, but never a sense of superiority. Always there is compassion. People may have flouted the rules of the essential order by, for example, becoming divorced or conceiving children outside marriage, but they never, for Willie, place themselves irretrievably beyond the pale. Open arms welcome them back into the ordered fold. He is glad to have the God in himself touch people and let them feel the divine support he has so valued for himself.

Above all Willie wants to show 'God's loving kindness.' He responds to 'loving kindness' with a serene enthusiasm. Many have spoken of his kindness and concern, people not as close as Ida, Branwen, Trevor and John. Others have complained of his obduracy and his blinkers over some issues, with some frustration, but no-one has spoken of an unkind act by Willie Simpson. 'Kindness is beautiful, spans the vale of tears. It is kindness that transmutes a residence into a home. Kindness is the hand, love is the heart. Kindness is the outward and visible sign. Love is the inward and spiritual grace,' he says.

My abiding image of Willie Simpson is of Wednesday morning conversations. I arrive to find the outer porch door a little ajar - I am expected. I walk through the hall and into the dining room at the back of the house. He is sitting with his back to me at the table by the window or in the armchair by the table, as likely as not working on a sermon. He is not aware of my arrival because of his deafness until I call, 'Good morning!' He insists on rising to greet me, the effort of rising from the low chair the only sign of his great age. 'And how are you?' I ask. Early in our acquaintance he would answer, 'All the better for seeing you, my dear.' Then, as the friendship flourished and we found our mutual sense of humour, I began to use his own words in answer to his enquiry when he was first to speak. This delighted him. Then we progressed to a silent, twinkling response with a welcoming smile, the answer implicit almost before the question crossed any lips. He does feel to me that he is all the better for seeing me, and I am in no doubt that I am all the better for seeing him.

Once out of his chair the movement is quick and purposeful. He scurries into the kitchen and switches on the kettle to make tea. The tray is laid and there is cake to eat, often rich Dundee cake, made by Mrs. Bowers of Chapel-en-le-Frith and likely delivered to his door by one of Bowers' red, green and white coaches which are to be seen about the district. It is good to watch him making the tea. All movements, hands opening cupboards, putting tea into the pot, getting cutlery from the drawer, stirring the brewing tea in the pot - all have an impulsive vigour and noise.The spoon rattles round the pot. The lid of the stainless steel pot is slammed to, a marked and curious contrast with the gentleness of his nature and the reticence of some of his exchanges. On the other hand there is a sense of unequivocal purpose in his actions, qualities plain enough in all the activities of his life.

There have been many Wednesday mornings together. I sit by the dining-room window, which looks south across the valley to Eccles Pike. In winter the low sun moves round, first catching my eye and then Willie's. As the sun follows its course he shifts his chair, first back and then forward to escape the strong light. The sun highlights his features in changing aspects. Whatever aspect, there is strength, not of granite, cold and unyielding, but of warmth and comfort. He sits towards the front edge of the chair, but leaning backwards so that his face is obliquely upwards, his long, broad nose and wide chin thrust forwards. His blue eyes are deep set, buried behind thick spectacles which magnify the eyes. Above them is an expanse of unfurrowed, serene brow. Issues occasionally disturb this serenity, such as concern about the financial future of Chinley Chapel, but the expression dissolves into sorrow rather than galvanises into anger.

The only time I recall seeing Willie suffering from lowered spirits was an occasion when he had had his ears syringed. He must have anticipated the outcome with pleasure, hoping to have some hearing restored, a relief from the irksome, frustrating isolation of deafness. However, the effect was to make him almost totally deaf. I had to resort to communication in writing. The pace of our conversation became painfully slow. It seemed to intensify the loneliness of deafness for him. He still attempted to make light of it, an indication, perhaps, that his way would be simply to accept and then deny - the means of coping learned very early. However, he was still amenable to suggestion that he should get better medical attention, the upshot of which was an improved hearing aid. To my great relief, he became accessible again, his spirits raised again and a full dialogue resumed. He looked heavenwards and smiled thankfulness.

I have imbibed the Simpson sermon for many hours. The real sermon is the life led by the preacher, as Willie would say himself. To follow a living person's life in the detailed and intimate manner demanded by a biography makes an alter ego. Is it 'fortunate', is it a 'coincidence' that our paths crossed at this time in our lives? (I have heard a friend say that there are no such things as 'coincidences', only 'God-incidences'). Three years after I dusted off a faith dormant for twenty years and came to a nonconformist chapel I met Willie Simpson. Then, as Chinley Chapel in the need of a minister found a minister in need of Chinley Chapel, so a life story came to a biographer. What is more, it is a blessing to come to be a friend of Willie Simpson, to know and to love him and to be loved by him. But is this really a co-incidence? Willie Simpson would not accept for a single moment any such co-incidence.

There was time when Willie did not want this story to be published in his lifetime. Now, with the approach of the seventieth anniversary of his ordination, an astounding, if not unique occasion, he has been persuaded that there are many who will benefit from the inspiration of his life story without waiting for his death to read it - not that, for Willie, is his death anything but the gate to unending joy. He is well prepared and hopes that when he does die we shall celebrate his life comprehensively. For the writer, it is inspiring and liberating to be able to write about him in the present tense. Willie Simpson lives - and will continue to do so long after his passing.

Sincerity

Now therefore FEAR the Lord and Serve Him in Sincerity and in truth - Joshua 24 verse 14.

It was 1959 that the Investiture of the Prince of Wales took place at Carnarvon Castle. Those who saw it on the Television were impressed by the Sincerity of the Prince. He convinced you that he was a man born to be King. He reminded you of another Royal Prince named Joshua. He successed Moses in the leadership of the Children of Isreal. One outstanding feature of his Reign was his "Sincerity" In the last days of his life he exhorts the people to "fear" the Lord and "Serve" him in "Sincerity" and in "Truth"

This man of God points out that if a child of God is to be a force in life he must be a translator of the noblest, an advocate of the soundest and a firm believer in God's great power. He needs to be crowned with Sincerity which is the essential for for the building of a fine personality.

Some say Joshua based his exhortation of Sincerity on the threat of "fear". We need to remember "Fear" in the Hebrew means faith, trust + confidence. Joshua was a wise man, he knew when he advised the Children of Isreal to develop Sincerity that it was the one spiritual characteristic which sustained, supported + and strengthed Man's personality.

It is interesting to note that Chinese Philosophers placed great stress on Sincerity. They believed that it was the basis of life, the foundation of life and the solid ground on which to build an edifice + They advocated that In wisdom desire soundness. In conduct desire squareness. In courage desire largeness. In care desire mindfulness These attributes can only be built on Sincerity. Do not let us forget that we need the help of God in the building up our lives. We cannot become an attractive personality without God's help. It is God within that displays God without. When our Sincerity comes bursting forth, it is then our "Sincerity becomes contagious," and thus we

The Church began when the people saw in Jesus his goodness, his holiness & his love. People hungered to be like him. Matthew left his tax gathering business, Simon the Zealot his politics & Peter & Andrew their fishing nets. The disciples became fired with Christ's spirit and in the spirit of sincerity they founded the Church.

In life you will meet the man who wants to say something in a bravo spirit that sounds rather sensational, for example, "Christ has had his day and the Church is a worn out institution" Let me declare as long as men & women remain sincere, Christ and His Church will never die but will live on and continue to do a good work in the world.

No sincere father will forsake his children No sincere workman will fail a good master and while men & women remain true, Christ and his Church will never cease but will grow in "favour with God and man".

There is a Contagion in the real & the genuine & the true. What is more contagious than a bright face, a firm step & a resolute will nobly displaying a sincere spirit

Let us not forget that Joshua was a Royal Prince who lived in the fear of God, lived in TRUTH TRUST & confidence in God. This spirit he lived throughout his life. There is no wonder at the end of his days that he should exhort his people, over whom he ruled, to serve God in sincerity and in Truth

Joshua that great spiritual saint & leader proved a great force in life among his people. His influence still lives on in US. Let us not forget that we all Christ's children, his agents & his workmanship. Let us so live that others may want to possess the same loving spirit that Joshua possessed. Let us so live that people may see not us but Christ who dwelleth within us. May we so live, true agents of Jesus Christ that we may warm the earth where e'er we tread.

Walk in the Lord that we may know
That fellowship of love
That we may find God's Joy & Peace
In Sincerity Divine

Amen.

Congregational Church,
MEXBOROUGH.

Ordination

— OF —

Mr. William Simpson
(Paton College, Nottingham),

to the work of the Christian Ministry and

Induction

to the Pastorate of this Church, on

Thursday, July 9th, 1925,
at 7-0 p.m.

Presiding Minister:
Rev. MODERATOR E. JOHNSON SAXTON.
Assisted by
Rev. Principal A. R. HENDERSON, M.A., D.D.
Rev. Professor H. F. SANDERS, B.A., D.D.
(Chairman, Notts. Congregational Union);
Rev. Professor J. G. McKENZIE, M.A., B.D.
Rev. W. D. EDMONDSON
(Minister, New Mills);
Rev. D. J. PRICE
(Minister, Chinley).

AFTERNOON SERVICE
at 3-30 p.m. Preacher

Rev. A. R. Henderson, M.A., D.D,

PUBLIC TEA at 5 p.m. Tickets 1/-. RECEPTION at 6-15 p.m.

Times Printing Co., Ltd., Mexborough.

Congregational Church

ENDERBY.

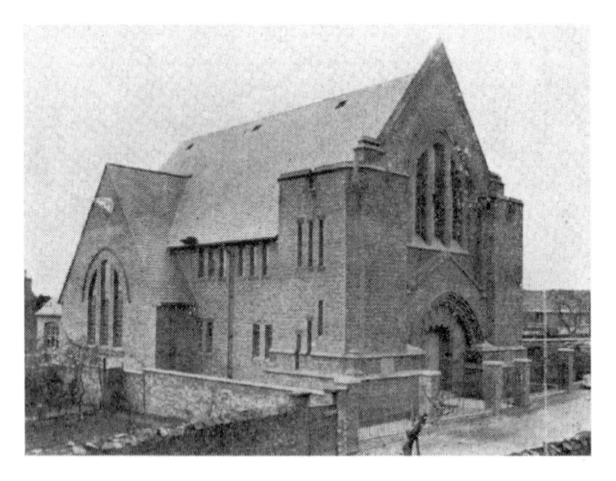

INDUCTION

TO THE PASTORATE OF THE ABOVE CHURCH OF THE

Rev. WILLIAM SIMPSON

(Late of Mexborough)

on

THURSDAY, JANUARY 24th, 1935.

RYECROFT CONGREGATIONAL CHURCH.

An Invitation to the

Welcome & Dedication

of the

REV. WILLIAM SIMPSON

(Late of Enderby, Leicester)

To the Pastorate at Ryecroft.

On MONDAY, APRIL 14th, 1947,

At 7-30 p.m.

To be followed by

GREETINGS to the CHURCH AND MINISTER.

BALLINGER & DEAN LTD., PRINTERS, WALSALL.

CHINLEY INDEPENDENT CHAPEL

(founded 1662)

Order of Service

and Invitation to the

Induction

of the

Rev. WILLIAM SIMPSON

(Late of Blakenall, Ryecroft, Walsall)

to the PASTORATE of CHINLEY CHAPEL

INDUCTION SERVICE 3.15 p.m.

WELCOME TEA - - 4.30 p.m.

to be followed by Greetings

to the fellowship at Chinley and the Minister

Organist: Mrs. N. ASKEY, L.R.A.M.

Saturday, September 11th, 1965

INDEX